The Life and Times of Miami Beach

The Life and Times of
Miami Beach

Ann Armbruster

Alfred A. Knopf   New York   1995

This Is a Borzoi Book
Published by
Alfred A. Knopf, Inc.

Published in the United States by Alfred A.
Knopf, Inc., New York, and simultaneously in
Canada by Random House of Canada Ltd.,
Toronto. Distributed by Random
House, Inc., New York.

Library of Congress Cataloging-
in-Publication Data
Armbruster, Ann.
The life and times of Miami Beach /
by Ann Armbruster.
p.   cm.
Includes index.
ISBN 0-394-57052-9
1. Miami Beach (Fla.)—History.
2. Miami Beach (Fla.)—History—
Pictorial works.   I. Title.
F319.M6A76   1995
975.9'381—dc20   94-11572   CIP

Manufactured in Italy

FIRST EDITION

Grateful acknowledgment is made to the following for permission to reprint previously published material:

American Play Company, Inc.: Excerpts from "Runyon Has Too Much Sand in His Shoes to Make Trip to Hollywood" by Damon Runyon (*New York American*, October 13, 1936), and excerpts from column "The Brighter Side" by Damon Runyon (*New York American*, May 14, 1937), copyright © 1964, 1965 by Mary Runyon McCann and Damon Runyon, Jr. Reprinted by permission of American Play Company, Inc., Sheldon Abend, President. All rights reserved.

BPI Communications Inc.: Excerpt from "Miami Beach: Dream Dump, U.S.A." (*Architectural Forum*, August 1959), copyright © 1959 by BPI Communications Inc. Reprinted by permission of BPI Communications Inc.

Paul Bruun, Jr.: Excerpt from a *Miami Beach Reporter* editorial by Paul Bruun. Reprinted by permission of Paul Bruun, Jr.

The Dreiser Trust: Excerpts from a series of articles by Theodore Dreiser (*Vanity Fair*, 1926). Reprinted by permission of The Dreiser Trust.

The New York Times Company: Excerpts from article on 1926 hurricane (*The New York Times*, September 20, 1926), copyright © 1926 by The New York Times Company. Reprinted by permission of The New York Times Company.

Will Rogers Memorial: Excerpt from "Carl Took Florida from the Alligators and Gave It to the Indianians" by Will Rogers (*Tulsa Daily World*, October 11, 1925). Reprinted by permission of the Will Rogers Memorial, Claremore, Oklahoma.

Time Inc.: Excerpt from "Coming On Down" (*Time* magazine, April 2, 1965), copyright © 1965 by Time Inc. Reprinted by permission of Time Inc.

University of Northern Iowa: Excerpt from "Miami" by Padraic Colum (*The North American Review*, Spring-Summer 1938). Reprinted by permission of the University of Northern Iowa.

For Gordon

Acknowledgments

Many people contributed their memories, photographs, expertise, and support to this project. In Miami, I am especially grateful to Helen and the late Bernie Baum, Chris and Barbara Hansen, James and the late Alice Wendler, Olive Delahunt, June Cutting, and Jenny Stapleton.

Dozens of people impressed me with their unique personalities and accomplishments as they shared their time with me. I'd like to acknowledge the late Patsy Abbott, the late Allan Albert, Art and Larry Apple, Leonard "Doc" Baker, Joanne Bass, Harvey Bell, Ken Benjamin, special consultant Seth Bramson, Richard Brown, Paul Bruun Jr., Diane Camber, the late Barbara Baer Capitman, Michael Carlebach, Laura Cerwinske, Charlie Cinnamon, Bea Courshon, Randall Cushing, Jimmy Destro, Doug de Witt, Michelle Oka Doner, Marjory Stoneman Douglas, Beth Dunlop, Henry End, Bill Farkas, Dorothy Fields of Miami's Black Archives, Peppy Fields, Ray Fisher, Neil Flaxman, David Fleeman, Mary Fleeman, Murray Franklin, Stephanie Oka Freed, Sandy Shapiro Friedland, Hal Gardner, Michael Gatti, Clark Geartner, Seymour Gerber, Buck and Adalea Goldberg, Deane Granoff, Henry Greene, Mel Grossman, Malvina Weiss Liebman Gutschmidt, Richard T. "Bud" Hart, Bill Held, the late Hal Hertz, Ira Hirsch, Tibor Hollo, Arthur Horowitz, Eric Jacobs, Mitchell Kaplan, Charles Kimball, Lisa Klausner, Don and Marge Klein, Michael Landwirth, Alan Lapidus, Morris Lapidus, Ken Laurence, Yvonne Lee, Rabbi Irving Lehrman of Temple Emanu-El, David Levenson, Nancy Liebman of the Miami Design Preservation League, Barbara Malone, Jim McDonnell, Pete McGovern, Mike Mersel, Hank Meyer, Polly de Hirsch Meyer, Aristedes Millas, Gary Monroe, Sid Morris, Phoebe Morse, Stephen Muss, Jack Ott, Dory Owens, Kay Pancoast, Arva Moore Parks, Billy Pine, Stan Platkin, the late Rocky Pomerance, Barry Ragone, Melvin Richard, Alice Rogers, Benard and the late Irma Rosenblatt, John Rothchild, T. Trip Russell, Eugene Scanlan, Dick and Ruth Shack, Fred Sherman, Betty Sherwin, Debra Sontag, Milt Sosin, Jay Spencer, Jewel Stern, Fred Tasker, Carol and Harold Unger, John Weiner, Michael Weiner, Paul Wimbish, the late Audrey Corwin Wright, Lisa Young, and Cyn Zarco.

I received endless research assistance from Becky Smith and Dawn Hugh of the research center of the Historical Association of Southern Florida; from Barbara Young in Art Services and Sam Boldrick and Victor Hernandez in the Florida Room of the Miami-Dade Public Library; from Steve Davidson of the Wolfson Media History Center; from Joan Morris and Jody Norman of the Florida State Photo Archives in Tallahassee; from John McMinn and the late Helen Purdy of the Richter Library of the University of Miami; from Howard Kleinberg and Joe Wright of the Miami News; and from curators at the Wolfsonian Foundation. Photographic assistance came from Doug Vann, Jennifer Kotter, Michael Germana, and Julius Sirillo.

Much appreciated advice on editorial, aesthetic, contractual, and emotional matters came from Ezra Doner, Esin Goknar, Vicky Gold-Levy, Thomas Hine, Betsy Israel, Hillary Johnson, Pam Kruger, Ellen Kunes, Eileen Lapsansky, John Margolies, Ron Meckler, Jane Nisselson, Bezu Ocko, Judy Prouty, Kitty Ross, and Penny Stallings.

For their guidance and enormous patience, I'm grateful to my editor, Victoria Wilson, and my agent, Melanie Jackson.

Special thanks go to my parents, Margaret and Bob, who first brought me to Florida; to my sisters, Julie, Peggy, Mary, and Betsy, who made it more fun; and to Darren, for sharing this project and so much else with me.

Contents

The beach was actually across the street.

The Life and Times of Miami Beach

Ocean Beach:
1900–1920

The steamer nudged into a wharf southward where we followed a board walk among white periwinkles and sandspurs to the two small casinos on the lower beach, faced by the great blue ocean. The beach stretched north in the sun haze between the stars of coconut palms and the curving, hissing whiteness of the shallow surf. The clamor of the small crowds by the casinos and the swimming pools was lost in the large winds, as the pelicans went over and the Gulf Stream laid against the horizon, beyond waves like pale-green glass.

—Marjory Stoneman Douglas, *Florida: The Long Frontier*

We walked, stepping gingerly and slapping at the mosquitoes, skirting the swamp going toward the Beach. An old alligator roared its resentment of our invasion of their age-old jungle. Mosquitoes blackened our white clothing. Jungle flies, as large as horse flies, waited for our blood. . . . The jungle itself was as hot and steamy as a conservatory. What on earth could Carl possibly see in such a place, I wondered crossly as I picked my way through the morass in my white shoes.

—Jane Fisher, *Fabulous Hoosier*

ROMAN POOLS and CASINO
MIAMI BEACH, FLORIDA

One hundred years ago, Miami Beach was an uninhabited peninsula that separated the Atlantic Ocean from Biscayne Bay and the frontier town of Miami. A fine, white-sand barrier beach stretched along the sea, fringed here and there with coconut palms, the legacy of an abandoned coconut plantation from the 1870s. Caribbean pines grew in the rich soil along a high central ridge in the center of the peninsula, but the rest of the land consisted of hundreds of acres of swamp—thickets of mangroves rising out of oozing black mire, squat cabbage palms, and clumps of a brutal, cactuslike plant called Spanish bayonet. Like many so-called wastelands, it was rich in animal life: oysters clung to the roots of the mangroves; barracuda, mullet, and snapper lived in a tidal salt creek; heron, ibis, and egrets waded in the shallows of the bay; ducks fished in the swamps; and raccoons nibbled sea grapes along the shore.

A visitor to Miami in 1895 wrote of an expedition to this deserted peninsula, landing on the bay side and walking over planks to the beach, then hiking up the sand to find a point where they could penetrate the jungle. As they slashed through what they thought was an overgrown Indian trail (in fact, relics indicate that native Tequesta Indians passed through around the fifteenth century), the safari party was startled by "a scream as of a woman in agony . . . a big tawny, fierce looking panther leaped from branch to branch a few feet away." Pushing on, they reached the Crocodile Hole, "a sinister, rather ghostly looking spot, dark with palms and oak in a tangle of lianas." Crocs, with their greenish, narrow snouts, lay about on the banks and in the water, easy marks for the sportsmen who sailed over from Miami's fancy Royal Palm Hotel to hunt them. On moonlit evenings, scavengers came to the beach to follow the tracks of huge loggerhead turtles, which crawled onto shore at night and laid nests of up to a hundred round, soft-shelled eggs. It was a highly lucrative adventure: turtle steak and turtle eggs were delicacies of the time. With few interruptions, that was life on the beach until the 1900s.

In 1870, a New Jerseyan named John Lum, while standing on the deck of a steamer returning from Havana, spied a few palm trees on the future Miami Beach shoreline and envisioned a fantastic coconut plantation there. He returned with a crew in 1882 to undertake a grand but miserably ill-conceived scheme; three years later, they virtually abandoned the scattering of coconut palms that had managed to take root to hordes of rabbits and the encroaching mangroves. His son Charles and his bride homesteaded on the beach, Crusoe-like, for a few years in the late 1880s, their closest neighbors six miles north in the House of Refuge for wrecked mariners. Then they packed up and moved to the mainland.

Two men saw a future in this daunting swampland. The first was John Collins, a pioneer in the American tradition. Collins, a New Jersey horticulturist, first came to Miami in 1896, determined to find out what had happened to the money he had invested in Lum's coconut plantation. After surveying the land, he was convinced that despite the coconut failure there

Before Collins Bridge opened in 1913 (the Venetian Causeway stands there now), visitors traveled to Ocean Beach via two ferries that departed from the foot of Flagler Street in Miami. The name Fairyland may have been inspired by Coney Island's Dreamland amusement park, then at its peak.

The Crocodile Hole, where visitors went on hunting expeditions. Before development, most of Miami Beach was covered with thickets of mangroves.

John Collins, 1927. A Quaker farmer from New Jersey, Collins, in 1909, at age seventy-one, bought more than a thousand acres of Miami Beach land to farm with subtropical fruits and vegetables.

was agricultural promise in Miami Beach. In 1909, at age seventy-one, he acquired 1,675 acres of the peninsula and established a farm on a strip of rich high ground west of Indian Creek. He very shortly demonstrated, to everyone's surprise, that mangoes, avocados, new Irish potatoes, Cavendish bananas, and other tropical fruits and vegetables could thrive in the middle of this jungle, in the middle of the winter.

Enter Carl Graham Fisher, an Indianapolis automobile baron about to turn real-estate developer. Fisher was a twentieth-century pioneer—he didn't settle land, he created it. By the time Miami Beach was incorporated as a town in 1915, Fisher had accomplished a good deal of the dredging, filling, platting, landscaping, and promoting that would soon turn the swampland into a boomtown.

Unlike communities that have been settled as refuges from religious persecution, as wilderness trading posts, or as experiments in utopian living, Carl Fisher's Miami Beach was basically a lark, a moneymaking lark. Yet creating the resort was nonetheless an extraordinary achievement, a fact that may be most acutely appreciated in Miami Beach, a place renowned in later years for fly-by-night schemes and scam artists.

• • •

Carl Fisher was an American original. He forged highways and built cities, driven by a sense of unlimited personal boundaries. He was also a product of his era, growing up on the can-do philosophies of writers like Robert Ingersoll and Horatio Alger during a time when the country was dominated by men like J. P. Morgan, Andrew Carnegie, John D. Rockefeller, and Cornelius Vanderbilt.

Fisher's own story is as fraught with obstacles as any Horatio Alger tale. He was born in 1874 and raised in a fatherless home in Indianapolis, supporting his mother and two brothers by the time he was a teenager. Despite having only 50 percent vision, a condition that went undiagnosed and uncorrected until he was thirty-one, Fisher painstakingly trained himself in athletics—he even learned to run backward and walk tightropes—and he raced high-wheeler bicycles before the craze turned to cars. But while Alger's virtuous boy heroes ultimately achieved success through a timely stroke of luck, Fisher seized opportunities. It was his good fortune to possess a love of speed and a talent for mechanics when an age of wheels was just beginning.

Fisher was energetic and colorful, a generous, domineering, daring, audacious, profane, hard-drinking, practical-joker "man's man." His child bride, Jane, saw her future written on a leather pillow in his bachelor digs: "A woman is only a woman, a good cigar is a smoke." He believed in middle-American values and conventions while routinely ignoring or defying them himself. He was innovative and instinctively entrepreneurial, pragmatic and brash, a sophisticated business-man and a social diamond in the rough. And he thrived on action. When Fisher was at the peak of his success in Miami Beach, he started another resort in Montauk, Long Island. Why, he was asked, when you don't need the money? Hell, he said, I just like to see the dirt fly. Fisher didn't need the money when he began work on Miami Beach; he was already a multi-millionaire from the sale to Union Carbide of his Prest-o-Lite company, which manufactured a headlight that ran on com-pressed gas. But the challenge presented by Miami Beach, com-bined with the potential for profit, made the project irresistible.

Promotion was a large part of the Beach's success, some-thing Fisher had an abundant talent for. As a teenager, he opened a bicycle repair shop—it was the beginning of the bicy-cle craze—and made a name for it by riding across a tightrope stretched between the two tallest buildings in town. When automobiles came in, he publicized his dealership and became a kind of local cult hero by floating around the Indiana coun-tryside in a stripped-down Stoddard-Dayton attached to a hot-air balloon. Spurred on by fellow automobile maniacs like Barney Oldfield and Louis Chevrolet, he used some of the profits from Prest-o-Lite to create the Indianapolis Speedway in 1909 as a testing ground for the latest technology, later turn-ing it into the country's best-known racetrack. He was also a leader in the good-roads movement. In 1913, seated behind the wheel of his Premier, Fisher blazed the way for the first transcontinental paved road, running from New York to San Francisco, to publicize the need for highways and to test their building techniques. The Lincoln Highway—named after one of Fisher's heroes—inspired other highway projects, including the north–south route Fisher undertook next. The Dixie Highway was less enthusiastically received, perhaps because of

its course through the deep South and its obscure destination, Miami.

At the time, Fisher was among the few people who could comprehend the deep effect the automobile would have on American life. He started work on the Dixie Highway almost immediately after he had begun developing the Beach, because he knew that although only an elite owned cars at the time, many more people would be able to afford automobiles in the near future and that drivers would go anywhere a highway could take them. Just as the cargo railroad had settled vast reaches of the United States—Florida, most recently—and the commuter rail had made once-exclusive seaside resorts like Coney Island and Atlantic City accessible to the nearby urban masses, highways would transform the American map as well as its way of life.

Fisher was aware that he was following in the footsteps of Henry Flagler, the cofounder of Standard Oil with John D. Rockefeller, who had carved out his own domain in Florida. Flagler had first visited the state on a honeymoon to St. Augus-tine and Jacksonville with his young second wife in 1883. Although he was long retired, there was something about the place that stirred his entrepreneurial instincts. He bought two railroads in northern Florida, formed the Florida East Coast Railway, and extended the line down the coast, reaching Key West just days before he died. Of course, providing a means of getting to Florida wasn't enough—he had to build places for the tourists to stay, so grand that they would be reason enough to come down, and each of the major stops along the line acquired a huge resort hotel. It was, in fact, the first time that tourism was the industry that developed a new territory (although that is now standard in most developing countries).

Flagler's St. Augustine showstopper was the Ponce de Leon, an enormous Spanish Renaissance fortress cast in concrete and coquina shell whose 540 rooms were wired for electric light, still a novelty in 1888. The Ponce was a fabulous gesture, but it never made money, and Flagler redoubled his efforts to make

Palm Beach, 240 miles south, "a magnificent playground for the people of the nation." There he built the Royal Poinciana Hotel, a giant, lemon-yellow, six-story frame building—the largest wooden structure in the world at the time. This monolith boasted seven miles of corridors, accommodations for 1,750 guests, a dining room so long, said writer Ring Lardner, it was "a toll call" from one end to the other, and 1,400 employees. With the opening of the smaller Breakers Hotel, Palm Beach quickly became the winter tarrying ground of the Eastern elite, another stop on their leisured rounds from New

When Carl Fisher, the Indianapolis automobile baron, arrived in Miami Beach in 1915, it was mostly mangrove jungle. By the time he died in 1939, Fisher had helped to underwrite the building of a city.

York to Newport, Saratoga, and Bar Harbor. A candid photograph taken at Palm Beach in 1896 perfectly describes this scene of wealth and privilege: the mansard roof of the Royal Poinciana fills the background, Cornelius Vanderbilt's private train is stationed in the middle ground, and informally arranged before it is a group of early visitors that included several Vanderbilts, a Townsend, a Bishop, a Cushing, a Whitney—turn-of-the-century Society in miniature.

Flagler intended Palm Beach to be the terminus of his line, but he was persuaded to extend the railroad to the raw frontier town of Miami by a woman named Julia Tuttle, a widow who'd moved to Miami from Cleveland after inheriting an enormous tract of land there from her father. A terrible cold wave had ruined most of the state's orange crop, the primary

cargo shipped on the East Coast Railway. In the aftermath of the freeze, so the legend goes, Mrs. Tuttle sent Flagler a bouquet of fresh orange blossoms to demonstrate that Miami was a frost-free zone. Truly subtropical weather and the donation of several hundred acres of land from Tuttle and other landowners in the area persuaded Flagler that pushing on to Miami would be a wise business decision.

The first train steamed into town in 1896. But by then Flagler had decided to extend the line all the way to Key West, and he had little time for Miami's civic welfare (although he did maintain a powerful hand politically). Flagler's crew, made up largely of black laborers, set to work cutting a grid of narrow streets into the land around the depot so that lots could be put on the market, dooming downtown Miami to its constricted layout. "Miami was no more than a glorified railroad terminal" to Flagler, huffed Marjory Stoneman Douglas in her autobiography, *Voice of the River.* "It's a pity that early Spaniards hadn't stayed here longer, because the Spaniards knew how to build beautiful cities. They would have put a great plaza on Biscayne Bay," the city's great natural asset. "It was magnificent," wrote Douglas, describing it as it appeared just a few short years before it was transformed by silt, sewage, and dredging. "There was turtle grass on the bottom, and the water changed its color from blue to green. There were schools of mullet jumping in the sunlight and flocks of birds turning and wheeling so their white wings would catch that light. You could see them far in the distance, shining as they turned, the egret and the ibis and all those wading birds we don't see now."

Flagler was wise enough to exploit this beautiful scenery for his Royal Palm hotel, situating it on the choicest waterfront spot, a point where the Miami River met Biscayne Bay. The hotel was another enormous rambling wood building with long verandas, surrounded by landscaped tropical gardens—"650 rooms tucked into a bower of flowers" as it was described by a Florida East Coast copywriter who had obviously never beheld its bulk, nor counted its rooms (it had 350). Like most of the millionaire's Florida hotels, the Royal Palm was painted Flagler yellow and trimmed in white; the long hallways were painted green and filled with white wicker furniture and potted palms. The tourist season was short—New Year's through Washington's Birthday—but it offered quite a spectacle for Miamians, with an opening-night ball, yellow-and-white surreys shuttling guests between depot and hotel, and a handful of luxurious yachts docked behind the hotel.

Although the Royal Palm got a small share of the rich and famous during the season, Miami had little of the social reputation that Palm Beach had. The city was regarded as a relaxed, sporting alternative to Palm Beach's formality—"a great place to go fishing," Flagler's company advertised. Not everyone wanted to go to Palm Beach, however, or was accepted there, and as the frontier town grew into a city, Miami attracted its own following.

Some of these tourists liked Miami so much they decided to build winter residences in a subdivision called Point View, which was being developed along the bayfront south of the hotel. Large homes went up on what is now Brickell Avenue (pioneer William Brickell's Indian trading post was once located there). Former Secretary of State William Jennings Bryan and his wife built a large home there—the Villa Serena—and so did Louis Comfort Tiffany and William H. Luden of cough drop fame. Carl and Jane Fisher, who had first happened upon Miami during a boat trip, purchased a Point View house by mail in 1910.

The Lummus brothers owned much of South Beach, which they touted as a great place for Miamians to build summer homes. To lure potential land buyers to auctions on the Beach, they advertised free china and glassware for everyone who attended. This photograph was taken by the first real-estate agent on the Beach.

Looking out across the bay, they could see what was simply called the Peninsula, a spit of swampy land with a long shoreline where Miamians went to swim. (Miami Beach became an island in 1924, when the land was blown away from a narrow isthmus called Baker's Haulover—Baker apparently hauled his boat over it to get to the sea—north of what is now 110th Street.) A tinny little ferry charged 5 cents to take passengers across the bay and drop them off at a landing at the southern end of the island; there they followed a raised boardwalk through the swamps—the mosquitoes "so thick that you had to have two hankies to fight them off"—in order to get to the beach and its two bathhouses, called casinos.

To amuse himself, Fisher explored the Beach on motorboat rides with an Indianapolis friend, John Levi, one day to be the city's mayor. "In the brackish waters, blue hyacinths impeded their progress. Vines and mangroves and the bristly little palmettos made dark colonnades," wrote Jane Fisher in *Fabulous Hoosier*, her 1947 biography of her former husband. A remarkable thing happened on one of these excursions, Jane told the author of *The Billion Dollar Sandbar*. (It is generally agreed that while not a reliable historian, Jane was a wonderful storyteller, and as one of her former friends defended her, "she only exaggerated stories you had no way of tracing.") Suddenly finding themselves lost deep in the tangled jungle, they came upon a small, impeccably dressed old gentleman who calmly advised them that "if thee continues thy way, thee will land in the Atlantic Ocean. So thee better turn around and retrace thy steps and thee will find thyself back in Biscayne Bay." This vision was John Collins, whom Jane always characterized as the Gentle Quaker, to his family's amusement. "He was anything but gentle," said Kay Pancoast, his grandson's wife. "He was a little firecracker, peppery as anything. He would say goodbye to his wife Rachel in the morning, go out to work in the fields on their New Jersey farm and not come back for weeks. He'd be down here in the meantime, and he'd go back and tell her all about it." It was probably that audacity that made Fisher interested in Collins and his new project—the construction of

a wooden bridge connecting the peninsula to the mainland. Collins had started the bridge as a means of transporting produce, but he also saw it as the first step toward developing his land into the kind of nice, respectable oceanside resort that lined the Jersey Shore.

The bridge, which reached halfway into the bay when Collins ran out of funds, piqued Fisher's imagination. It was clear that Miami would attract more and more tourists like himself, who would be enchanted with the extraordinary subtropical landscape and weather, and he knew from the example of New York's Brooklyn that oceanfront property would become more valuable as the city of Miami grew. He was certainly in a position to make a good deal, since the landowners on the Beach were ambitious but underfinanced. Without deliberating long, he lent Collins $50,000 in 1912 to complete the bridge and received in return a strip of about 200 acres running from ocean to bay. Then he cultivated two bankers from Miami, the brothers J. E. and J. N. Lummus, who owned 580 acres of land on what is now South Beach, at the southern tip of the peninsula. They'd begun their own real-estate company, Ocean Beach Realty, with this homespun pitch: "Pure air, unexcelled climate. Come to Ocean Beach every year. Buy a lot and build a winter home." Fisher lent $150,000 to help them improve their holdings and acquired 210 of their acres. Now, with a sizable chunk of swampland in his possession, he had something to play with.

Jane Fisher wrote that her husband took a stick and drew a little plan for the city in the wet sand—"Look, honey, I'm going to build a city here! A city like magic, like romantic places you read and dream about but never see." In principle Fisher's plan for making land seemed simple enough—cut down the mangroves, cover with silt and sand dredged up from the bottom of the bay, let dry, and voilà—but in fact the job turned out to be a five-year, money-eating "mammoth phantasmagoria," according to Jane. Clearing was the most arduous job. Black workers, most from the Bahamas and Mississippi, were plagued by mosquitoes as they stood hip-deep in mud

TOP LEFT: *Miami Beach, circa 1920. Workers chopped down the mangrove swamps to prepare the land to be filled.*

BOTTOM LEFT: *On the horizon a dredge pumps up marl from the bottom of Biscayne Bay to be spread over a cleared portion of land. Will Rogers later called the dredge "the national emblem of Florida."*

BELOW: *Dredge pipes spewing out the foundation for exclusive Miami Beach property. The piles in the background are topsoil, which was spread on the fill after it had settled and dried.*

OPPOSITE: *To illustrate the impressive development of Miami Beach, Fisher assembled his work teams in front of the Nautilus Hotel for a publicity shot. At center stage were elephants Rosie and Carl, who became town mascots. On Sunday mornings in the twenties and thirties, Rosie pulled schoolchildren down Lincoln Road in a fringed, high-wheeled cart.*

and hacked away at the wet, fibrous wood of the mangroves; finally, a specially designed tractor equipped with a machete-like blade was shipped in to pull out the trees by the roots. Once enough sand had been pumped in to cover the leveled mangroves, it was left to dry and solidify in the sun. Then the ground was covered with a layer of topsoil hauled in from the Everglades. To prevent the soil from being blown away, groups of women and children planted sprigs of Bermuda grass by hand. Gradually the man-made city acquired a colorful landscape assembled from the world over. In her book, Jane Fisher included this slightly fantastic, time-compressed description of how the sandy wastes were soon transformed by

> bougainvillea, orchid trees, poinciana, hibiscus, and the thousands of oleanders—white, rose, apple-blossom pink and deep red—whose perfume became the very breath of the new paradise. Thousands of coconut trees and stately royal palms and feathery Australian pines outlined the avenues and boulevards that as yet existed only on blueprints. The Australian pines shot up fourteen feet in one year to clothe the Beach with their glorious foliage. Small trees with trunks as dainty as fawns' legs hung heavy with papaya melons. Avocado trees drooped their rich, dark globes. Oranges were as large as grapefruit, and lemons as large as oranges. All these, planted at the same time, grew evenly. Within six months the Beach burgeoned into horticultural magnificence . . . overnight our man-built paradise was discovered by choruses of singing birds and brilliant clouds of butterflies. . . .

As each section of fill was finished, roads were marked off, limestone laid down in the roadbeds, and the necessary utilities installed. Fisher was also busy dredging up more fill from the bay and creating small new islands from scratch—Star and Belle islands first, later the Sunset Islands.

It was all a much more expensive proposition than Fisher had ever imagined. He'd first estimated that laying the foundations for a city would cost him $75,000, but the dredging alone turned out to cost $52,000 a day, and filling just the lower portion of the beach took a year and a half. Visitors to the beach surveyed the vast sparkling whiteness that had replaced the swamps and wondered if Fisher had gone mad. Why pour a fortune into the creation of land when so much uninhabited Florida acreage was there for the taking?

But as the project ballooned, Fisher only poured more money into it: "When you've got a bull by the horns and he's going downhill you can't let go," he explained to a colleague. He installed a golf course and a yacht basin ("Oh my god, honey, I forgot about all the boats!" he exclaimed one day) and

Fisher paid homage to his idol, Abraham Lincoln, at every opportunity: he blazed the first cross-country highway and named it after him, then gave the name to this 1914 hotel, the first luxury accommodations on the Beach, located on Lincoln Road, the intended Rue de la Paix of the South.

put up a grandstand on Biscayne Bay where people could view his new annual regatta. He built the Lincoln Hotel on one end of Lincoln Road, his future Rue de la Paix, and a glass-enclosed tennis court at the other.

Despite these jazzy improvements, no one was rushing to buy lots on Miami Beach, the name the town was incorporated under in 1915. Eventually Fisher was driven to offer free lots to those who'd build substantial structures on them, and only got a handful of takers. The problem seemed to be that Fisher's idea was simply ahead of its time. "Miami Beach and Carl himself seemed unreal to our visitors," wrote Jane. "They would go away shaking their heads. 'It can't last,' some of them said. 'It's too purty.'"

World War I interrupted the Beach's development, and after it, everything changed. Fisher took a new sales tack: instead of offering discounts to buyers, he guaranteed that his company would raise land prices 10 percent every year, ensuring

investors that property would become more valuable. "When a thing doesn't sell," he said, "raise its price." More important, he stopped trying to promote the Beach as a genteel retreat for wealthy businessmen—or at least he dropped the genteel-retreat aspect. That type of place was not only out of sync with the restlessness the war had created, it was out of character for Fisher—and one key to the continuing success of Miami Beach was the ability of its developers to identify with their customers' tastes. Sports, action, were in Fisher's blood—Miami Beach was going to become a sportsman's paradise. Gone were the appeals to the "old folks," Fisher said in an interview in *Business* magazine in 1923.

To inaugurate his new era, Fisher introduced polo to the Beach, a perfect choice because polo combined speed with snob appeal. He established the first polo field off Lincoln Road, and later converted a World War I airfield into four fields. A barn was built that could shelter 220 ponies and bunk 100 grooms, and alfalfa, white clipped oats, timothy, and Para-

Club House and Polo Field, Miami, Fla.—22

With the arrival of the rich, land began to sell. The introduction of polo to Miami Beach in 1919 was Fisher's ingenious idea.

grass hay were shipped in from Indiana. He put up a half-timbered, Tudor-style clubhouse and grandstands, although many polo enthusiasts—the men in jodhpurs, the women in long pastel dresses and oversized hats—sat on top of their cars and watched from the perimeters of the field. Fisher loved to play, too, though he personally disdained any polo-ish pretensions and rode a horse called Old Jerry.

Some think that the introduction of polo was the turning point in the Beach's success. Pete Chase, a personable Key Wester who sold real estate for Fisher from under an umbrella beside Collins Bridge, reported that he made his first big sale, a lot for $20,000, right after the first polo ponies came across the bridge. (Fisher invited the woman over for a bottle of champagne.) Polo attracted the kind of people Fisher wanted to sell houses to. To paraphrase bank robber Willy Sutton, he realized that rich people was where the money was.

Will Rogers was a frequent visitor to Miami Beach during the twenties. In a 1925 column, he attributed its success to

Carl G. Fisher, the man that took Miami away from the Alligators and turned it over to the Indianians. Had there been no Carl Fisher, Florida would be known today as just the Turpentine State. If you were an admirer of Turpentine, why, naturally, you would go there. Of course it would have always attracted the true disciple of this perfume laden fluid. But Carl drained off the water-moccasins, the blacks, and the Turpentine, and replaced them with a Hotel and New York prices. He put in a Jazz Orchestra and one-way Excursions; advertised free heat the year 'round; fixed up the chug-holes so the Fords could get in; rehearsed the mosquitos 'till they wouldn't bite you until after you bought; shipped in California oranges and tied 'em on the trees; whispered under his breath that you were only ninety miles away from Palm Beach, with its millionaires and its scandal.

15

Johnny Weissmuller;
Jack Ott, the Aqua Tot;
and Pete des Jardins at
the Roman Pools, 1929.

Miami Beach:
The Twenties Explosion

If there is no scenery, as in Florida, we make it, and when there is, we sell it. . . . In other parts of the world resorts are exploited as resorts. Here they're exploited as real estate developments.

—Anne McCormick,
The New York Times, 1926

The beachfront north of Twenty-third Street in its natural state.

Although hundreds of acres had been developed by the end of World War I, most people who lived on the Beach still lived in "town," the area between Biscayne Street, which traversed the southern tip of the peninsula, and Fifth Street. The owners of most of this property, J. E. and J. N. Lummus, had hired a local character named Doc Dammers to auction off their land from the back of a wagon, and they finally began to have some success when they threw free crockery and pocket watches into the deal. The Lummuses had come to Miami from a small Georgia town—"Scratch every third Miamian and you'll find a Georgian," old-timers say—and they couldn't give a hoot about Fisher's plans for a fancy winter resort. The Lummuses advertised South Beach as a great place for a Miami family to build an inexpensive summertime home, and they welcomed anyone who was white, law-abiding, and could afford the property payments. Soon a few modest bungalows dotted the empty streets. With their sloping roofs, heavy masonry walls, and broad verandas, the bungalow style, an Indian building form interpreted by the English, was particu-

larly appropriate for the scorching South Florida summers. J. N. Lummus's rather substantial bungalow home, "Salubrity," was something of a landmark.

The Beach got its first hotel in 1912, a simple, wooden two-story building at Ocean Drive and First Street, called Brown's. There were bedrooms on the second floor and kitchens on the first, available in combination or singly. Malvina Weiss Liebman Gutschmidt's family stayed there for a while after they moved to Miami Beach from New York in 1920 for relief of her mother's asthma. "The Beach was like a South Sea Island then," she said. "We ate all our meals right on the beach, practically lived on the beach. We'd pile up driftwood and ferns and burn them at the full moon. We swam in the phosphorescence and fished all day—my brothers wove their own cast nets. Once we knocked the bottom out of a butter tub and had

South Miami Beach, 1921.

glass put in at a car repair place. We'd dive off our little row-boat and put the bucket in the water and it would magnify everything so we could spear the fish more easily. My brother could see the ripples the fish made from the shore—sometimes he could even tell from the ripples what kind of fish they were."

Hardie's, Smith's, and Cook's casinos thrived on the pennies they collected on admissions and bathing suit rentals from Miami day-trippers. Sheriff and casino owner Dan Hardie thought bringing the circus to town would attract even more customers, and asked Carl Fisher to contribute $500 to a circus fund. Fisher promptly offered him $500 to keep it away. Sophistication was arriving in the form of the Roman Pools, Fisher's new casino built at the Twenty-third Street site of the Pancoast family's homely Miami Beach Pools and Casino, a simple shingled building with a driftwood interior. In its place went a block-long, onion-domed pavilion sprouting shiny brass flagpoles and fluttering pennants. Planted on the beach behind it was a picturesque windmill that pumped saltwater into two long swimming pools. Stores and tearooms occupied the ground floor of the casino building, ballroom-dancing instruction was given in the second-floor meeting hall, and diving and swimming exhibitions were held at the pools. The proper hour for ocean bathing, according to the standards set by Palm Beach society, was 11:30 in the morning. Although styles would be revolutionized within a few years, women around 1920 still wore thick two-piece suits, long black stockings, and bathing shoes, with scarves or mobcaps covering their long hair, and no man would have dared expose his naked chest. Afternoons at 4 p.m., a bugle call brought casino-goers to the sands for a half-hour physical culture class led by Professor McCarthy, a local eccentric and fitness buff whose regimen included the queer practice of marching up and down Ocean Drive rhythmically swinging his arms (today he would have plenty of racewalking company). Besides running a gymnasium at Smith's casino in South Beach, McCarthy peddled a special suntan lotion—his secret recipe turned out to be mineral oil and iodine—that he concocted in his bathtub, leaving behind a permanent ring for his angry landlord.

There were only 644 permanent residents on the Beach in 1920, and all eighty phones could be listed on one page in the Miami telephone directory. "It was like living in a big park, quite beautiful and more or less untended," said Kay Pancoast, who came here in 1924 after she married John Collins's grandson, architect Russell Pancoast. "Mother and Dad [Pancoast] had a charming white concrete house at the end of Lake Pancoast. They had a cistern under the whole house so they could

Hardie's, Smith's, and Cook's casinos, as bathing pavilions were called, catered to visitors from Miami. Admission was 5 cents and swimsuit rentals were a quarter.

Winter Bathers at Miami...Jan., 1921.

keep their water, but for a long time they had to take a boat to the mainland to shop—a spool of thread took a great deal of planning. By '24 there was a grocery store way at the tip of South Beach, and Mr. . . . oh dear, I forgot his name . . . would come around every morning to take your order and deliver it in the afternoon." It was a friendly, quiet life. Locals could drive miles along the oceanfront, park their cars at the ends of the deserted streets, and have barbecues on the beach in perfect solitude. Children took their fishing poles along on the school bus to Miami so they could fish off the side of Collins Bridge while the driver chatted with the bridge tender. On Christmas Eve, everyone was invited to a community party at Carl's glass-roofed tennis court, where a present for every child in town lay beneath an enormous fir tree.

Empty of houses, the streets Fisher had laid out cut a grid into the sparkling sands baking under the sun. But the years of pioneering work were beginning to show results. A few big homes were turning up among the spindly Australian pines, built by some of Fisher's midwestern industrialist friends, often referred to as the "kings" in their fields. John Hanan, the shoe king, built an imposing residence across the street from the Fisher home on Fifteenth and the ocean in 1916. Way, way up on Forty-fourth Street and the ocean James Snowden, the motor oil king, built a Beaux Arts–style mansion with classical detailing

Diving exhibitions, alligator-wrestling matches, and beauty contests were held around the saltwater pool (the windmill pumped the water in from the sea) at Carl Fisher's Roman Pools and Casino. This exhibition took place about 1928.

A stuffed alligator was a favorite prop in tourist photos.

The Life and Times of Miami Beach

The Whale Club, Miami Beach, 1922.

Louis F. "Red" Snedigar, the mayor of Miami Beach, 1927.

Interpretive dancers, 1924.

A public exercise class at Smith's Casino, 1924.

The Beach's love affair with lights began in the twenties, when the first grand hotel, the Flamingo, featured a glass dome illuminated at night in red, green, and gold.

on a huge estate perfectly landscaped for a mid-western city. Harvey Firestone, rubber king, bought the estate in 1921.

As land sales picked up, Fisher realized that the city needed a big new hotel to house prospective buyers. Boxy Lincoln Hotel, on Lincoln Road, with its stuffed crocodile heads over the front desk, was just too rustic.

The future lay in the Flamingo Hotel, on Biscayne Bay, which opened on New Year's Day, 1921. Although no one had invented this term yet, it was Miami Beach's first Hotel of the Year. It satisfied all the requirements: it was big, it was expensive, and it had a theme. Fisher, who had become enchanted with flamingos on a trip to Andros Island, painted the hotel pink and commissioned flamingo murals and plaster reliefs for the lobby. From a modern perspective, the 150-room, $2-million Flamingo resembled its graceful namesake in color only. It was an austere and hulking building—a competitor of Fisher's once remarked that all of Fisher's hotels looked like barns. Its most impressive feature was a dome illuminated by red, then green, then gold lights. But what the Flamingo lacked in architectural distinction it made up in variety. The hotel had a yacht anchorage, an Oriental tea garden, tennis courts, private cottages, shops, a men's club, a broker's office, and a barn for the forty Guernsey cows that supplied hotel guests with fresh milk during the season. Never mind that there were still no water mains to the Beach.

MIAMI BEACH VS. CORAL GABLES

It was clear after the war that Miami and Miami Beach were going to start growing fast; Marjory Stoneman Douglas, a columnist at the Miami *Herald* at the time, recognized that the area was at a turning point in its development. "I hammered away on the idea that Miami Beach should build a great boulevard along the ocean beaches," she wrote in *Florida: The Long Frontier*, "that new streets should be wide, with parkways and shade trees, and that land everywhere should be set aside for parks and recreation places, and that there should be housing regulations and zoning. It was a shock to realize that no one was interested in anything but that both cities should grow larger."

One notable exception to this trend was George Merrick, the developer of Coral Gables on Miami's west side. He and Fisher would have the most profound effect on the area in the coming years, but they approached development from almost opposite directions. Fisher took a laissez-faire attitude to planning, whereas Merrick held to the idealistic philosophy of the City Beautiful movement. Around the time that Fisher was propping up skinny little trees along the Beach's neat, Indiana-style grid of streets, Merrick was putting together a master plan for a middle-class suburban utopia on the other side of town. Coral Gables's design—by Phineas Paist, a landscape architect and artist—featured graceful, tree-lined parkways, impressive city gates, plazas, fountains, neighborhoods full of Mediterranean villas, a zoned business center, even a university.

Fisher was no such cosmopolitan. If he had articulated an approach to city planning, it probably would have been similar to his thoughts on education. Who needed these fancy private schools opening on the Beach that taught subjects like French and Latin? he wrote a friend. "Teach a child to read and write and do arithmetic and his own mind will figure out what it's best suited for." For his own child, Miami Beach, he did only what was necessary to sell it as a residential resort. He filled in the land, provided power and water, landscaped, built hotels and sports facilities to feather the city's nest, and then left it to grow into itself.

Until 1933, when Miami Beach adopted municipal zoning regulations, developers determined any planning requirements on the basis of what would help sell property. To ensure the uniformity that investors liked, Fisher's companies prohibited commercial development in residential neighborhoods and set minimum cost requirements for houses in different areas on the Beach. (The highest was $15,000, for homes along the ocean

and on Pine Tree Drive; the lowest was $5,000, for homes in the Sunset Lake area, in the center of the island.) Fisher's own hotels went up on the bay—where their massive silhouettes were visible from Miami—or inland, rather than along the oceanfront. But he wasn't saving the beach for the public; he wanted to reserve those prime sites for the homes of the wealthy. A public road ran along the oceanfront north of the Firestone Estate until 1924, but as land began to sell, the Fisher interests petitioned and won the right to move the road

several hundred feet west, creating a strip of choice lots but robbing the public of access to that part of the beach. And while the Lummus brothers sold the city Lummus Park, on the ocean in South Beach, stipulating it for permanent public recreational use, and Collins donated land for Collins Park between Twenty-first and Twenty-third, on the ocean, Fisher built private golf courses.

The results of the two developers' approaches unfolded over time. Miami Beach did find what it was good at, and in the

Miami Beach: The Twenties Explosion

The Nautilus Hotel garden, 1924. The afternoon tea dance was a 1920s institution. Local women came in hats from the Blue Hat Shop; their dresses were purchased at clothing salons owned by Madame Louise, Madame Claire, and Madame Moghabghab.

succeeding decades far surpassed Coral Gables in fame. It also grew up and out and wild with buildings, in outright defiance of zoning regulations and contrary to anyone's idea of what a playground should look like, including Fisher's. "Miami Beach is growing into a big, ugly city," said Jane Fisher in a 1968 interview. "I don't think it's what Carl would have wanted." Coral Gables, meanwhile, has remained a stable community and a model of city planning. Its property values have consis-

tently been among the highest in the city, while Miami Beach is recovering from a long depression.

Most people agree that among Miami's founding fathers, George Merrick has a higher historical quotient than Fisher. Merrick loved Florida, a contemporary of both men once wrote; Fisher would probably have loved as well any place where he could have made a lot of money. Fisher himself admitted that Miami Beach was primarily a business venture for him. In a tribute to him years after the city was established, someone referred to the Beach as Carl Fisher's dream. "Wasn't any goddamned dream at all," he snapped. "I could just as easily have started a cattle ranch."

"He was just a businessman," said Mrs. Douglas, dismissing Fisher. And yet in an era when business, advertising, and the magic of motion pictures was transforming the country, Fisher was a businessman-adman-showman extraordinaire. His flamboyant personality and appetite for excitement set the style and pace for Miami Beach and its later developers.

Dredging the bottom of Biscayne Bay for landfill made it deep enough to allow yachts to anchor. Here, yacht owners watch Fisher's annual regatta, photographed in the mid-twenties. Speedboats were the millionaires' latest fascination.

FLAGLER STREET, 1925

Building the Flamingo turned out to be a wise decision. Fisher built other big hotels in the next few years, and he soon needed them, for by the mid-twenties, Miami Beach was at the heart of a statewide land boom of enormous proportions. The Florida boom was a harbinger of the stock market explosion of 1927–1929, and it would parallel both its overnight success stories and its disasters.

In several respects, Fisher was largely responsible for setting the boom in motion. Flagler had opened the state to development by constructing the East Coast Railroad and building hotels along the route. Fisher, acknowledging Flagler as his inspiration—one of the first projects he undertook was the creation of a memorial to him—opened the door to Florida even wider by building the Dixie Highway, which would eventually run from Montreal to his new winter resort, Miami Beach. As Fisher foresaw, the family automobile was a fact of life by the twenties; by 1925, when the boom was at its height, assembly-line innovations had brought the price of a Ford with self-starter down to $290, and surveys showed that more families had a car than a bathtub. Car infatuation combined with a shifting perception of the world after the war. People were eager to play and see new things. A kind of travel fever came over the country, and Fisher was right there to help steer Americans to Florida.

Although it seems commonplace now, Fisher's come-on to the public—ocean bathing in the middle of winter—was a startling and seductive idea in the twenties. New Yorkers hurrying home in the freezing January weather saw the message "It's June in Miami" blazing above them on a Times Square billboard. Reams of press-release poetry about the beauties of the Beach appeared in full-page newspaper ads,

beneath an illustration of "a tropical paradise with castles towering among the stars and voluptuously-attired semi-Eastern, semi-Italian ladies and gallants drifting . . . in spacious gondolas," according to an account of the time. Fisher's publicity office bombarded the tabloids with photos of comely young women in daring one-piece bathing suits and rolled stockings (or even—gasp!—no stockings) or such typical sights in wonderland as children using an elephant as a diving board.

Fisher's first big publicity coup came shortly after the opening of the Flamingo, when he enticed the wildly popular President-elect Warren Harding to come down to "straw-hat land" for a visit. Fisher had imported an elephant sometime earlier to use in publicity photos, and now he got Rosie rigged up to caddy for Harding on the golf course. The picture that appeared in newspapers across the country fixed Miami Beach in the public's mind as a place you had to see to believe.

But a great sales campaign doesn't work just on graphics and gimmickry; it has to embody a concept. With his "uncanny knack for spotting trends," as his first wife put it, Fisher sensed a desire among plain, hardworking, middle-class Americans for glamour and luxury, and he created an image for the Beach—rich, selective, romantic, sexy, playful, sporty—that appealed to these new tastes (countless other real-estate developments of the twenties, in Florida and elsewhere, tailored the formula to their own needs). He advertised the Beach as the American Riviera, the home of "America's wealthiest sportsmen, devotees of yachting and other expensive sports," and "palatial," "luxury," and "exclusive" became boomtime catchwords. "Live like a millionaire in a millionaire atmosphere"—the expression came from a Miami Beach brochure of the fifties, but it was Carl Fisher's idea in a nutshell and it was the key to the Beach's success for several decades.

With the physical and conceptual groundwork accomplished, Fisher rode the wave of "Coolidge prosperity" that followed World War I. Money came pouring in from successful investors who thought it might be more profitable to put

The once-plebeian suntan gained new status in the twenties, cultivated by American expatriates vacationing on the Riviera and popularized by the discovery that the sun was a source of vitamin D.

The Life and Times of Miami Beach

Fisher's people managed to entice President-elect Warren Harding down to the Beach for a pre-Inaugural vacation. Pictures published in national newspapers of Rosie the elephant caddying for Harding (not shown here) put Miami Beach on the map.

their capital into Florida real estate than back into stocks, and from working-class adventurers whose imaginations were fired by stories of fortunes made overnight in Florida. "One Good Investment Beats a Lifetime of Toil," read a sign in a New York real-estate office; beneath it was the account of a young man who'd made $500,000 in Florida in four weeks: "Say! YOU can do what George Cusack, Jr., did!" A *Liberty* magazine story on Florida made famous this example of boomtime one-upmanship: "That's nothing! I parlayed two quarts of synthetic gin into $75,000 in eight months!"

After the stock market began its sharp climb in 1924, Florida was besieged with buyers, sellers, speculators, builders, con artists, and hangers-on who'd drained their hometown savings accounts, packed their belongings in storage, and headed south to find their fortune. A long-defunct local newspaper, the Miami Beach *Beacon*, described them in this way in 1927:

> The boomers of 1925 were as representatively American a crowd as could be assembled. There were seasoned promoters from Los Angeles and Hollywood in their Rolls-Royces or their flivvers, according to their previous luck in booms. There were prospectors and oil wild-catters from Texas and Oklahoma. Conservative bankers from Ohio and Indiana rubbed elbows with skeptical tight-fisted folk from New Hampshire and Vermont. "De quality" and "poh white trash" came in equal proportions from all over the south. Approximately half the population of Georgia moved bodily across the State line, and the doubled police force of Miami, it was harshly charged, was recruited from tall hill-billies who had never before seen any form of auto except a flivver engine running a portable sawmill. Soda jerkers, shoe clerks, and gunmen from Chicago gave up their normal professions for real estate. No matter what a man had been, he opened up a real estate office when he hit Florida, and was soon talking glibly of key lots, commissions, proposed hotels, closings, abstracts, exclusive listings, resales and predevelopment prices, as one to the manner born.

Miami was at the center of the statewide boom, and boasted the brightest developments—Coral Gables, the largest single subdivision, and Miami Beach, with the choicest pieces of property. Single lots on the Beach were typically going for $20,000 to $25,000, up to $50,000 for the best lots— "positively insane prices," wrote Theodore Dreiser, reporting on the boom for *Vanity Fair* in 1926. One man who had paid $800 in 1914 for a lot at the corner of Collins Avenue and Fifth Street sold it for $150,000 cash in 1925.

The area's growth was enormous: Miami's population had leaped from 30,000 in 1920 to 75,000 in 1925; over the same period, the Beach grew from 644 to 15,000. Visitors poured in—more than 2,000 people a day arrived in Miami by train—and one pastime was clocking cars on the Dixie Highway. In 1925 and 1926 alone, 1,366 subdivisions were plotted in Miami's Dade County. By July of 1925, the city had issued 5,917 real-estate brokers licenses and was putting out sixty more every day. "The routine of incoming real-estate operators was stripped down to bare essentials," wrote Kenneth Ballinger in *Miami Millions*. "They alighted from the train and looked about for someone who knew his way out of the depot. 'Is this Miami?' usually was the first question. Then, 'Where can I rent an office?' 'What is the price of acreage?'" Real-estate advertising made the newspapers balloon. The Miami *Herald*, whose ordinary weekday edition could run to 88 pages, printed the greatest amount of advertising in 1925 of any paper in America, and the Miami *News* published a 504-page edition in 1925. "I'd like to take the *News*," one woman told a subscription salesman, "but I'm afraid it would fall on me."

A housing shortage forced people to sleep in the parks, to rent space on front porches, to put up tents on lawns and along the highway. But no matter where they slept, in the daytime everyone showed up on narrow little Flagler Street, downtown Miami's main drag and the headquarters for dozens of real-estate offices. The atmosphere was saturated with noise from the clatter of riveters constructing the requisite boomtime sky-

Room hunters on the Miami Courthouse lawn, 1925. During the boom, midwesterners flooded into Miami. Construction couldn't keep up with the demand for accommodations; a spot on a porch could go for $25 a week.

scrapers and from the cars that rattled down the street day and night, horns blaring as people overflowed the sidewalks (the city had to issue an ordinance prohibiting people from selling real estate in the street, too). Some developers hired marimba bands to play in front of their offices to help draw in customers.

Inside the sales offices, prospective clients could inspect blueprints and artists' depictions of such future beauteous communities as, say, Moro del Gold Fish or Vista del Porpoises, as Dreiser dubbed them, and sample in the office decor the luxurious life that awaited them. "The rugs, the flowers, pictures, maps, grandiose wicker furniture, desks, mirrors," marveled Dreiser. "By far the greater majority of the smaller hotel lobbies and club entrances could in no way compete with them." No less impressive were the real-estate salesmen themselves, "or realtors—as they so nobly dub themselves—in their light smart clothes and swaying their palm leaf fans."

In the lower echelon of salesmen were the notorious

"binder boys," young men who turned speculation into a kind of boomtime sport. The binder boys paid a small amount for a binder, or option, on a piece of property; the binder was then sold and resold many times, each time with a profit built in for the seller. By the time the first payment came due, the price of the land was enormously inflated. Binder boys working the Miami Beach market stayed at the Fleetwood Hotel, giving rise to the peculiar boomtime expression, "Are you married or living at the Fleetwood?"

All across the state, large parcels of real estate were selling sight unseen. Sometimes there was no road to the land, sometimes there was no land, just swamp. Not infrequently, buyers bought a lot where there was, as yet, only water. Cars heading north on the Dixie Highway carried signs that said "Don't go to Florida. Don't get robbed." Northern newspapers printed editorials critical of the boom, if only to stanch the flood of money leaving their own states. Theodore Dreiser wrote that

Crowds, even mobs, were everywhere during the boom. The Miami Bank and Trust Co., December 23, 1925.

he was "nauseated" by the flimsy, crass character of Florida and the false promises of its developers.

Before I reached Florida, my truthful author's tongue was hanging out in anticipation. Ah, I said to myself, what a treat I have in store for me! I will take gondolas and glide to the exclusive verandas of clubs, palaces and pleasure pavilions . . . have dinner in the sunken gardens, perhaps, and later dance in the Louis Quinze ballroom and then, after a day of bathing in the blue sea in sight of those many svelte beauties displaying themselves under striped awnings or parasols, I will move, a little regretfully but still hopefully, on to the next wonderland. I will. I will.

What he discovered, of course, was that for the most part, this gay world did not exist. Instead, he found "predevelopments" filled with pine trees and swampgrass.

Miami Beach was among the few places that didn't disappoint Dreiser.

These avenues are, for the most part, lined with such houses as are advertised—all borrowed from Hollywood, California, by the way—and all charming. Here the patio, the oriental flat roof topped by the brilliantly striped awning, the fountain, the private swimming pool, the private yacht moored at one's very door, flourish at their picturesque best. . . . And sunshine and hibiscus and startlingly colourful and intriguing hotels and apartment houses—each with its private pier or yacht basin, its jazz orchestra, its mass of nosing cars—humanity eager to spend and to bluff and to show off and upstage. And, by day—wellformed girls in bathing suits and smart capes sportively trundling hoops with sticks along the principal residential streets. And the winter sport—male or female, in his or her flannels and best car, rolling here and there.

• • •

Paul Whiteman's dance orchestra, the most famous in the country (photographed here in Coral Gables's Venetian Pools), was a fixture in Miami. Performances featured numbers like "When the Moon Shines Over Coral Gables," "Miami Shores," and "Tamiami Trail."

BOOMTIME ARCHITECTURE

The Spanish trend predominated—the mellow walls, the iron fretwork, the pools gleaming in the palms, the tiled staircases leading to blue water.
                                    —*Fabulous Hoosier*

The "Hollywood" homes of Miami Beach are still there, acres of them west of Collins Avenue, some still grand, many, especially the smaller homes, slightly dilapidated. These houses have become part of the Beach's landscape, taken for granted the way the Deco hotels of South Beach once were. But like the Deco buildings, homes in the Mediterranean Revival style, as it is now called, are monuments to the mood and tastes of a particular time and place.

They have red, or sometimes blue or green, barrel-tiled roofs, arched windows, front doors decorated with wrought-iron grillwork, spindles, maybe a phony coat of arms. An entrance loggia borrowed from a medieval cloister may have been enclosed to make an extra room. New homeowners sometimes discover a floor of unglazed tile or rock-hard Dade County pine beneath the former owner's moldy carpeting. Up on the high ceilings, a decorator's coat of spring-green paint might conceal beams of wormy cypress, a wood favored in the twenties for its ready-aged look. Many homes have bathrooms with their original brilliant polychrome tiles still intact, looking straight out of the twenties but for the lucite accessories or color-coordinated toilet paper. Bedrooms have French windows that open onto decorative but useless balconies where decades of housepaint chips have collected, or onto second-story sun terraces, an inexpensive feature thrown in to appeal to twenties sun-worshipers. In those pre-air-conditioning days, concrete-block houses were insulated from the heat by heavy plaster-and-stucco walls, and the best had large, high-ceilinged, cross-ventilated rooms. Sometimes, too, these houses include features that tell of the inexperience or haste of boomtime architects and builders—most houses were completed four or five weeks after their foundations were laid, while even a modern tract home would take about eight weeks. A fireplace may be adjacent to the front door or a garage turns out to be barely big enough for a Honda, much less a car with a running board.

All these little homes were inspired by the Mediterranean Revival style invented by Addison Mizner for his wealthy Palm Beach clients. When Mizner arrived in Palm Beach in 1918, guest of sewing machine heir Paris Singer, the growing resort town was filled with oversized "cottages" painted Flagler yellow and white. Singer commissioned Mizner to come up with some kind of style that would match the setting better than these northern imports; the only stipulation Singer made was that the building couldn't be yellow. The resulting building was everything but yellow. Mizner took a basically Spanish architectural style and blended into it whatever historical element might strike his fancy—an English hall, a Venetian Gothic window. Artfully arranged and carefully aged, the resulting hybrid looked both fantasy-driven and can't-put-your-finger-on-it authentic. His next commission from Singer, the Everglades Club, made Mizner the darling of Palm Beach socialites. A mansion by Mizner became de rigueur, and each was more outrageous than the last. The "Bastard-Spanish-Moorish-Romanesque-Gothic-Renaissance-Bull-Market-Damn-the-Expense Style," as it was dubbed by Mizner's biographer, Alva Johnson, inspired the imagination of builders and developers all over the state.

On Miami Beach, the neoclassical Beaux Arts style of the 1917 Firestone Estate became history fast. The boomtime mansions that went up in the choicest Miami Beach locations—along the oceanfront, on Star, Palm, and Hibiscus islands, on North Bay Road, on Pine Tree, Indian Creek, and La Gorce drives—adopted Palm Beach magnificence. Carl Fisher's second home, on North Bay Road, detailed in a 1925 article, was designed by Miami architect August Geiger "to represent an Italian villa of the Renaissance period" with a landscaped sunken garden. "Famous Florentine villas" provided the inspiration for the main rooms, with their carved, hand-painted wood ceilings, walls hand-plastered in blue and gold, and teak floors, a fitting setting for the $30,000 pipe organ covered in tigerwood Fisher said he would install in the living room.

A large rectangular tower adjoined one corner of the house, which Fisher had had built as an observation point for prospective customers. From there they could see all the lights of Miami across the bay, the new causeway that connected the two cities, and a sweep of land covered with clean, white, stucco-covered Spanish casas, Italian villas, and Moorish palaces, most buildings a combination of the three. Although the smaller homes were actually fairly inexpensive to build (even with the mansions, the damn-the-expense part generally came in the furnishings and special additions), they always included a few picturesque details that seemed rich in historical pedigree. Exteriors were aged by applying three or four coats of different-colored paint, allowing the base colors to show through. Chimneys were contrived to look as if the stucco had crumbled off with age, exposing the brick beneath. Floors were said to be made of "age-enriched Spanish tiles, not . . . less than 200 years old."

The choice to use historical European architecture was partly a reference to the Spanish settlement of Florida in the sixteenth century. But it was primarily the theme-park environment that appealed to Florida's twentieth-century settlers. This quasi-historical architecture lent an air of romance and grandeur to the brash new Florida frontier. In *Only Yesterday*, a history of the twenties, Frederick Lewis Allen suggests that this taste for a fantasy lifestyle—which also showed up in California's Mediterranean-style developments, in the half-

A typical Mediterranean Revival–style house, popular in Miami Beach and much of Florida in the twenties. Shown here: the living room and an interior hall and stairway.

OPPOSITE: *The Palm Beach–like mansions that went up along the oceanfront, each with its stretch of private beach, had all been demolished by the seventies, as Collins Avenue was developed with apartment buildings and hotels. The Leon Sigman Estate.*

timbered Tudor homes of the suburban Northeast, and in urban Gothic office buildings—developed as a reaction against the rough world of big business that had brought prosperity. The radically changing times provoked a drive to escape "into the easy-going life and beauty of the European past, into some never-never land which combined American sport and comfort with Latin glamour—a Venice equipped with bathtubs and electric ice boxes, a Seville provided with three eighteen-hole golf courses."

Beach romantics were particularly fond of a Venetian touch. Sometimes it came in the form of Venetian gothic details incorporated into the architecture, but usually it meant gondolas and barber poles at water's edge. For years one of the most popular postcards of Miami Beach featured the picturesque home of artist Henry Salem Hubbell on Dade Canal (the waterway John Collins dug to barge his produce out to the bay), with its barber poles, the family gondola moored alongside. The gondola craze started when Jane Fisher had one sent back from Venice. Carl had his boatbuilder make copies, suggesting enthusiastically that his Bahamian gondoliers wear lobsters around their necks. Jane relates a somewhat glorified version of the Beach's Venetian love affair in *Fabulous Hoosier*.

Painted gold and circus-red, and carrying musicians with guitars and mandolins and sweet-voiced singers in Venetian costumes, these gay craft drifted through the canals and the lagoons of Miami Beach. The little sailboats for hire on Biscayne Bay were set with red, henna and turquoise sails. Italian troubadours in gay costumes strolled around the Roman pools, singing and playing.

The Life and Times of Miami Beach

LEFT: *The architecture and customs of Spain and Venice were freely interpreted. This private house captured the imagination of photographers for decades.*

OPPOSITE: *Carl Fisher's main competitor in Miami was George Merrick, who developed Coral Gables. The subdivision's best-known landmark was the Venetian Pools, a favorite site for promotional gimmicks. Former Secretary of State William Jennings Bryan would stand on a platform suspended over the pool and deliver an eloquent sales pitch for the city, for which Merrick paid him $100,000 a year.*

WHERE TO STAY

Miami Beach, the Mecca of the whole world, lacks sufficient accommodations for the thousands who are pouring into this iridescent spot of gold and sunshine.

—Real-estate advertisement, 1926

Florida boosters liked to claim in the twenties that the state would soon be a center of business and agriculture, but it was clear that its future was as a resort. Florida wasn't just a new destination—it had the corner on a new holiday season. Although only a handful had been able to take a winter vacation before Fisher's experiment, it was becoming almost as popular as a summer vacation. Builders rushed to accommodate the waves of tourists. By 1925 the Beach had thirty-three hotels as well as eighty apartment buildings and hundreds of private homes. Although a few of the mansions from the twen-

ties remain, all of the Beach's great boomtime monuments—the hotels—have been demolished (the restored Coral Gables Biltmore is now the only local example of their immensity).

Among the most outstanding were the Hotel Pancoast, built by Collins's son-in-law, Thomas Pancoast, just a lot away from the pioneer's home and next door to the modest seaside hotel that the Wofford family had built in 1921. The Pancoast held the distinction of being the most expensive in the city for many years. An early pamphlet noted its "atmosphere of Old Spain," where waitresses wore costumes of Spanish peasants, and an aviary in the inner court was filled with tropical birds.

The Flamingo got some competition when the Fleetwood opened on the bay. A fifteen-story pile of horizontal planes and jutting rooflines, the Fleetwood resembled a deck of cards being shuffled. A postcard listed its vital statistics: accommodations for 700 guests, a roof garden seating 800, a dance floor 230 feet long. The hotel was also the home of the most pow-

erful radio station in the country at the time, WMBF—Wonderful Miami Beach, Florida—installed by Jesse Jay, the son of the inventor of the auto vacuum tank, Webb Jay. Jay later established radio station WIOD—Wonderful Isle o' Dreams. Another hotel, the Floridian, "252 rooms and 252 baths," went up on the bay at Sixth Street in 1925, "in the Italian Renaissance type of architecture."

Fisher pulled out the stops for his Nautilus hotel in 1923, a massive building whose four wings took the form of a Greek cross. The entrance was reached by a baroque double sweeping stairway flanked by enormous carved stone columns. The interior was typical South Florida Spanish: tile floors, wrought-iron chandeliers, massive fireplaces (the mantel adorned with a miniature Spanish galleon, perhaps), Persian rugs hung over balcony railings. Lobbies were furnished in gaily upholstered furniture, an array of tables and plant stands, and boldly patterned carpets. Guests could have lunch under the awning on a deep terrace furnished with rattan chairs, the sun slanting in through the balustrade. There were three tennis courts and several small cottages scattered about the grounds; one was called the President's Cottage, should any president deign to visit. It was surrounded by Washington palms. Two small islands, John's and Collins's, an homage to the pioneer, were connected to the hotel property by an ornamental bridge whose columns were carved to represent Miami Beach sporting events.

Smaller but equally tony, perhaps, was the sixty-room King Cole, favored by the English polo teams Fisher paid to play on the Beach, and by other polo enthusiasts. Dressed in their jodhpurs and riding boots, the polo crowd served themselves kidney pie from the breakfast sideboard in a dining room decorated in "a particular rustic design with ornamental and heraldic features of the eleventh century," according to a 1925 report in the Miami *News*. Among the regulars were a certain Marquis of Waterford and one Lord Cromwell, who noted that Americans are "extemely more serious about polo than are

Englishmen . . . they ride so fast and so hard—veritably like mad. . . . Possibly it is because they are so young, so enthusiastic, so RICH." According to Jane Fisher, some of their equally rich countrymen bought property on the Beach and paid the appraisal price of the land when tax time came instead of the taxes.

The Deauville was built in 1924 by a former salesman of Fisher's who struck it big and drove around in a Rolls-Royce. Joe Elsener's hotel was an unremarkable, utilitarian building, but, as in much contemporary resort architecture, what it lacked in style it made up for in size. The Deauville had the biggest dining room, the biggest gambling room, but most notably, the biggest pool—100 feet wide and 165 feet long, nearly one million gallons, with a four-level diving platform. Gertrude Ederle, the first woman to swim the English Channel, was engaged to give exhibitions at the pool the first two seasons. A day band and a night band performed at a poolside pavilion, and guests could be directed in sun ray "sun cures" and physical culture classes. Unfortunately, Elsener spread himself too thin, and the location—way up in the wilderness at Sixty-third Street and the ocean—was too remote. When the Depression hit, the hotel closed. It was finally sold in 1934 to a former showgirl named Lucy Cotton Thomas Magraw, remembered for her habit of shaving her head at her husband's request. Lucy Magraw renamed the hotel the Beautiful Deauville and tried and failed to make it run off the profits from its gambling room. She then leased the hotel in 1934 to Bernarr Macfadden, physical culturist, food faddist, and publisher of tabloid journals, including the New York *Graphic* and *True Confessions*, who operated the Macfadden-Deauville as a "health hotel." When Macfadden celebrated his marriage at age eighty to his forty-four-year-old third wife, Johnnie Lee, carrot juice and carrot cake were served beside the million-gallon pool.

Second to Fisher on the Beach was a developer named N. B. T. Roney. Roney paid $2.5 million for the Roman Pools and the hotel site next to it—a few years earlier, Fisher had been offering to give that lot away to anyone willing to build a luxury hotel on it. The massive Roney Plaza, which was surrounded by fifteen acres of formal gardens and a 1,500-foot waterfront, featured a two-story-height lobby and a replica of the Giralda Tower in Seville (the Giralda Tower was very popular that year, showing up at the Coral Gables Biltmore and the Miami News Building downtown, all three designed by the New York firm Schultz and Weaver).

Roney also created Espanola Way, off Washington Avenue, two blocks of residential and commercial buildings built to resemble an old Spanish village in miniature. Espanola Way had weathered stucco façades, wrought-iron balconies and red-tiled roofs, rickety wooden shutters, bright striped awnings suspended from spears, pseudo-gaslights, courtyards, and wishing wells. To cap off the Spanish effect, Roney even hired dark-eyed girls to drift about with shawls and fans.

Guests were entertained by "day" and "night" bands from the pavilion beside the Deauville Hotel's million-gallon pool.

According to a local newspaper account of the time, the Spanish Village was inspired by some visiting New Yorkers who "mentioned that with all the tropic surroundings of the Beach there was no place where an artist would feel the same atmosphere as he would in Greenwich Village in New York or in the artist quarter in Paris." It was foreseen that the atmosphere of the Spanish Village would inspire businessmen to discover their underlying artistic temperament, but in fact the little hidden street soon went to bootleggers—you could buy a quart of booze at Tom and Mac's Tomac shoeshine parlor—and later to bookie joints and tacky rhumba studios. Perhaps it simply took time to grow into itself, but Espanola Way has indeed become a little Bohemia in the heart of Miami Beach where "the European custom . . . of sipping the cooling draught while idly watching the activities in the thoroughfare in front of the sidewalk tables" has finally taken hold.

One of several boomtime monuments, the Roney Plaza was the pre-eminent Beach hotel in the thirties and forties. It was built on land Fisher had once offered to give away to anyone willing to put up a million-dollar hotel on it.

The lobby of the Nautilus, 1924. Attracting rich Europeans to the Beach was a serious preoccupation. The former Mrs. Carl Fisher wrote her ex-husband requesting reservations at the Nautilus for an acquaintance "reputed to be the sixth richest man in London . . . he is the real thing and only the best accommodations will be suitable."

As the boom proceeded, the proposed projects became more and more fantastic. Given the dimensions of the development so far, perhaps they seemed plausible. Most of these schemes never made it further than blueprints. A theater was planned for the Beach, the Temple Cleopatra, a Greek temple flanked by giant Pharaonic-animal figures. Architects drew plans for a hotel on six acres of Belle Isle that would have dwarfed even the enormous Roney. Most outrageous of all was a developer's plan to add twelve more islands to the three man-made Venetian Islands, all to be connected by a causeway called the "Drive of the Campanile." Developers advertised that a Venetian-style bell tower would be constructed at the center of each island, and bronze bells would ring at set intervals all down the way. Development-happy locals did put their foot down at the idea of Biscayne Bay being filled in with land, however.

Coral Gables was not immune to this madness. Developers there announced plans for a $9-million hotel, The Towers, to be built in the shape of a four-pointed star along a frontage nearly a quarter mile long. Included in the plan was an enormous glass pavilion based on the Crystal Palace, a private chapel, a private theater, and a man-made beach (there is no natural beach in Coral Gables), as well as special facilities for the ailing—a hospital wing staffed by nurses, doctors, and surgeons, and climate-controlled dining rooms appropriate for different blood pressures.

In Palm Beach, Addison Mizner had moved from architect to master builder. He planned to put his own construction company to work building a Spanish-style development called Boca Raton, "the world's most architecturally beautiful playground," where no structure could be built without Mizner's personal approval. Among the city's planned features were such amenities as a 1,000-room hotel, an air terminal and a yacht basin, gondola-covered lakes and waterways, a Spanish Village, a polo field, a casino, Irving Berlin's Cabaret, and a Pirate Ship Cabaret. Less generic features included the choice of ten Mizner-designed model homes, and, most

unusual, a subdivision for blacks. The pièce de résistance of Boca Raton would have been Mizner's own home, a twelfth-century-style Spanish fortress designed for an island in the center of Lake Boca Raton and reached by a working drawbridge. Unfortunately, Mizner completed only a couple of blocks of his vision for Boca Raton when the bottom fell out of the boom.

WHAT TO DO

Gone was the community of sober businessmen Fisher had once angled for—or, at least, its members were content to party once they hit Florida, with perhaps an occasional visit to Thomas and MacKinnon, a brokerage firm housed in an elegant oceanside mansion. The city was a favorite resort now for a new crop of American commerce kings, from malted milk to steel manufacturers. "The rich newcomers . . . bought land, built palaces, spent like mad people," wrote Jane Fisher, lamenting the good old days when neighbors would come over for sandwiches, lemonade, and a sing-along. Now suppers were given for thirty, and tea dances for three hundred weren't uncommon. "I know of one dinner party that cost twenty-eight thousand dollars. The beautiful new city, in fact all Florida, was like a mighty vacuum sucking in all the loose money in the world."

Miami's quiet atmosphere was becoming raucous, and the behavior of its nouveau riche tourists drew almost as much contempt as it would in the fifties. "This is a paradise of the recently rich," a *New Republic* article described Miami in 1924.

Palm Beach, of course, is where truly sanctified Society may be found, but from those royal sands the timid automobile magnate or accessory king from Detroit or Cleveland usually flees to Miami rather than risk a snubbing. These innocent souls pursue the standardized recreations of their class. They

The twenties' urge to live in another land and time inspired a number of whimsical projects. Among the few that were realized was developer N. B. T. Roney's Spanish Village, designed to add a bit of old-world charm to money-mad Miami Beach.

Like so many others, the Hotel Venetian Island never made it further than the blueprint stage.

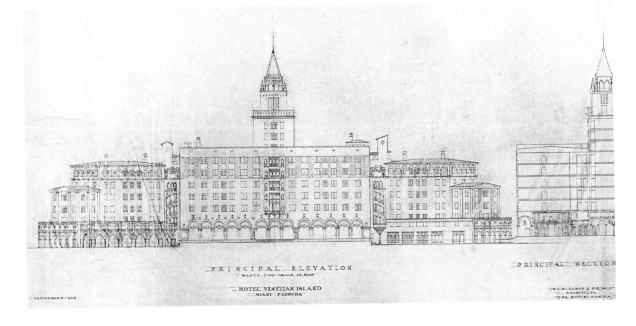

PRINCIPAL ELEVATION

HOTEL VENETIAN ISLAND
MIAMI FLORIDA

PRINCIPAL SECTION

motor, they play bridge, the younger ones dance, and unanimously and hugely, they play golf. Miami has new golf courses oftener than New York has fresh murder-mysteries. Most of them are bad, but if you are fat, fifty, and a Grand Rapids furniture king you don't mind. You array yourself in white linen knickers, like a small circus tent, an Angora jacket in need of a shave, a saucy cap, and dark goggles. Thus attired, you go out happily into the sunshine and swing your clubs.

This was not the crowd for subdued relaxation. Sports was part of the "go spirit" that had Americans in motion in the twenties, and exploiting the taste for the hearty outdoor life was essential, Fisher discovered. "I had been going after the old folks," he said in a 1923 interview in *Business* magazine. "I saw that what I needed to do was go after the live wires."

A promotional pamphlet for the Beach in the twenties called it America's Greatest Year-Round Outdoor Playground: the Motorist's Mecca, the Fisherman's Paradise, the Golfer's Ideal, the Surf-Bather's Joy, the Yachtsman's Rendezvous, the Tennis Player's Dreamland, the Horse-Lover's Utopia. Miami Beach was now on the circuit for polo teams, even if Carl Fisher sometimes had to pay to get them there, and swimming stars, such as Olympic champion Johnny Weissmuller and Jackie Ott, the Aqua Tot, regularly performed at the Roman Pools. John Oliver La Gorce, the publisher of *National Geographic* and an early supporter of the Beach, sponsored the La Gorce Open, which brought down golfing stars Gene Sarazen, Bobby Jones, and Tommy Armour. On the Beach's four golf courses "one can hit the little ball within view of the Atlantic or along cool inland canals." Or, as so often happened on the

Downtown Miami, 1921.

45

The start of an outboard race at the annual Biscayne Bay Regatta held in front of the Fleetwood Hotel, 1931.

"Aquaplaning" for publicity in Biscayne Bay. The Flamingo Hotel is in the background.

course off Lincoln Road, one could send stray balls flying past shoppers on the sidewalk. Tourists getting golf lessons were accompanied by a caddy who carried a gun filled with "liquid poison" to douse mosquitoes that fed on the pupils. Golf mania led to all sorts of curiosities. Promotors of the suburb Hialeah, which drew on local Indian imagery, advertised Seminoles as "ideal golf caddies" because of "their marvelous eyesight trained for years in the impenetrable fastnesses of the Everglades." When ordinary golfing got boring, tourists could try night golf, in which balls were coated with "radiopaint" to make them visible, and some hotels set up "obstacle" golf games—simple miniature golf courses—on their lawns.

A bus service took tourists from the Beach to the horse races at the Miami Jockey Club, which opened every January 17 for a meeting of fifty-one days, seven races a day. The fact that Miami was the only place for midwinter racing in America accounted for the influx of gangsters and gamblers into the area that would have such a profound influence on the city's growth. A man known as Ace-Deuce Solomon, for instance, who rose to the top of Miami's gambling hierarchy in the fifties, came to town during the boom to run a jitney line out to the track. Seeing that everyone was asking him for tips, he realized that bookmaking on horses would be more profitable than driving and formed a syndicate for taking horse bets. Betting was also rampant at the boxing matches held regularly at the Olympus Theater in downtown Miami, under a dome studded with a tropical moon and stars.

Fishing of course was a mainstay. In the twenties, there were more than two hundred kinds of fish in Biscayne Bay alone and dozens of other varieties farther out in the Atlantic. A promotional pamphlet of the time described some of the most common as the "great, leaping tarpon; the savage barracuda; the powerful bonita; the quick-dashing king fish; the darting, many-colored dolphin; marlin; the deep-diving grouper." Filling in the sports gaps: fox hunting to hounds, horseback riding, archery, and archery-golf, "a game whose star is just now in the ascendency."

MIAMI VICE

If anyone wants to go to hell in a hurry there are greased banks aplenty in Miami. —Reverend R. S. Wrightman, as quoted in *The New York Times,* March 9, 1925

Miami and the Beach showed that wide-open atmosphere in the twenties that still characterizes South Florida. Rum-running was considered a fairly respectable occupation during the early years of Prohibition. Limousines lined up at the wharfs to welcome the boats laden with bootleg liquor that came in from Havana, Bimini, and Nassau, and people drove off with their "fish" neatly wrapped in brown paper. Bootleggers landed whiskey on the beach and drove it over the causeway at night. What was $18 a case in Bimini or Nassau sold for twice that in Miami. Shipped north in refrigerated railroad cars, under cover of grapefruit or tomatoes, it could sell for $100 a case.

In a situation that foreshadowed the catch-up game played today between drug smugglers and the Florida Coast Guard, rumrunners attached surplus "Liberty" engines manufactured for World War I airplanes to specially designed boats that could outstrip any Coast Guard craft. The favored thirty-four-foot boat equipped with two Liberty engines could go 25 mph loaded, and in a pinch, 45 to 50 with the goods thrown overboard. Coast Guard officials occasionally captured and confiscated the boats (although Prohibition agents sometimes let the runners use them long enough to earn back their investments) and began to add them to their own fleet in order to keep up with the runners.

Rum-running turned nasty as the twenties progressed. In one notorious incident in February 1926, the King of the

Florida Smugglers, Duncan W. "Red" Shannon, was shot to death after a high-speed chase. Coast Guardsmen spotted him cruising near the county causeway toward dusk and set off after him as he made a run for the Flamingo Hotel yacht basin. When Shannon refused to stop, officials opened fire near the hotel dock. Guests at a tea dance watched as Shannon died on a mattress on the hotel lawn.

Most of the big hotels openly served liquor, and a well-known beer garden operated on a main street on the Beach, shielded from view only by a bamboo blind. Customers came to have an iced beer, one of the most prized Prohibition drinks, and to listen to the gramophone. "Huts mushroomed in the palmetto forests," wrote Theyre Weigall, an English journalist who published a book about his experiences in boomtime Miami. "It became smart to drive around at midnight to these palm-thatched dens to gamble and drink bad liquor sold at exorbitant rates." Wrote Jane Fisher, "People said slyly, 'I feel like hell—I was out in the jungle last night.'" Among the most notorious Prohibition revelers was Carl Fisher. He had always had a taste for liquor, but, like so many others, it took the Volstead Amendment to get him really interested.

Several big gambling casinos opened, most run by local men. For years a Miamian named John Olive had run the Seminole Club in Miami's old Fort Dallas, whose doors were open only to the patrons of the Royal Palm Hotel across the street. Then Bill Dwyer, the biggest beer baron in the country, built the Palm Island Club on residential Palm Island, over the protests of neighbors. Big-name entertainers performed there, and men came in white tie and tails to play at the gaming tables. A man named Art Childers arrived in Miami from North Carolina and became manager of the Floridian Hotel. Childers helped Detroit gambler Mert Wertheimer establish a casino nightclub with a big patio fronting on the hotel lawn; the opening-night show featured Eddie Cantor, Jack Benny, Sophie Tucker, and the dance team of Cesar Romero and Nitza Bernelle. Public pressure forced the casino to close, but it was allowed to reopen on the top floor of the hotel. Patrons

entered by taking the elevator up nine floors, climbing a flight of stairs, knocking on the door of a hotel room, and passing through a closet to enter the gaming room.

Prostitution flourished. "On Flagler Street of an afternoon may be seen large quantities of too beautiful ladies, too young, too exquisitely dressed," wrote *The New Republic*. "Later in the evening, if you know how to get in, you may see these same ladies, in Tower-of-Jewels evening gowns, at Miami's few and exclusive gambling resorts, throwing away thousands of furniture-and-automobile-magnate dollars."

Dreiser despaired of Miami's materialistic atmosphere.

The yachts! The houses! The cars! The "Rolls." "Where's that head waiter?" "What do you want to bother me now for with that scheme? Cantcha' see I'm out for the evening? Call Jack and tell him to get the yacht. I've got twelve lined up and more coming. But Friday we gotta be back for the races, see, sure. Talk to me then. If I win, I'll be easier." And the nightclubs, the dancers, the free and open gambling, drinking, prostitution in the private rooms. Money, money, money! And yet with all of those weary, dreary crumb-pickers in those wretched down-and-out houses near the business heart.

Oh, I loathe it all. All.

Yet despite the flimsy character and the phony pretensions that Dreiser and some other visitors abhorred, the Beach had an indisputable vitality.

THE RICH AND FAMOUS PHOTOGRAPHED IN MIAMI

"Now and then one ran across a reputed millionaire from somewhere," wrote Dreiser of boomtime Florida in a 1926 *Vanity Fair* article, "now and then a celebrity of the social, stage or motion picture world—Al Jolson, Will Rogers, Gloria

Swanson—but where exactly will one fail in these days to encounter a celebrity, or two, or three?" Miami was one of the few places in Florida that did not need to exaggerate its celebrity patronage. Photos from the local historical archives are evidence. A sample from the twenties includes pictures of:

Rose O'Neill, the inventor of the Kewpie doll, posing with her creation in the garden of the Flamingo Hotel.

Babe Ruth throwing a ball during the Yankees' spring training in Miami Beach's Flamingo Park.

Carl Fisher playing the net at the Flamingo Hotel tennis court.

Roger Firestone posing with his terrier and model ship.

Jane Fisher wearing saddle shoes, a hat, and a shirt with a crisp white collar, standing with her mother-in-law under a palm tree.

President Warren G. Harding, January 29, 1921, on the golf course, smoking a cigar.

Child swimming star Jackie Ott in his white admiral's suit and cap, chest out, looking bored; Jackie, circa 1922, being pulled behind Gar Wood's speedboat ("If Dad said do it, I'd do it," Ott recalled).

Colonel Green in his roadster, top down, Pekinese dog standing on top of the backseat.

Mrs. Charles Kettering, wife of the vice president of General Motors, a.k.a. the Empress of Dayton, a stout and serious older lady, sitting in a carved stone chair in the courtyard of the Pancoast Hotel.

Jack Dempsey, former heavyweight champ, looking over a plat in a Miami real-estate office. Young men crowd behind him, smiling. People in the back of the room are standing on chairs and desks to get a view. In the background the distinctive craggy face and round glasses of H. H. "Honk Honk" Arnold, the city's first traffic director, who initiated the system of one-way streets in downtown Miami.

Al Jolson sitting in a canoe on the beach with a microphone the size of a dinner plate, with chorus girls from a Broadway show. Each of the young women is wearing the sash of a local

subdivision—Miami Shores, Hollywood, Miami Beach, Coral Gables, Boca Raton, Atlantic Shores.

Show promoter Tex Rickard and his infant daughter, holding herself up by a shovel, breaking ground for the Miami Beach dog track, October 20, 1928.

Bobby Jones and his father about 1926. Dad is wearing a short paisley tie and plaid knickers and has a big cigar in the corner of his mouth. Bobby is handsome, black haired, wearing a white shirt and knickers, knee socks, and two-toned golf shoes. Bobby leans on his putter, Calamity Jane.

Gentleman Gene Sarazen in a tie and white shirt, smiling as he wings a club. A medal hangs from his belt loop.

"Yeast king" Julius Fleischmann with his golf club and a cigarette. He's wearing a knitted vest, his shirt open at the collar, white flannel pants, and two-toned shoes. He is unsmiling, fierce, the sun in his eyes.

Shimmy star Gilda Grey—"beginning to show the despoiling effects of time," wrote one observer—posed on the roof of the Flamingo. She wears a striped one-piece suit, her hair wrapped in a scarf, leg coyly bent. A wrap coat with a huge shawl collar slips off her shoulders.

Glenn Curtis, aviator and developer of Miami's Arabian fantasy subdivision, Opa-Locka, posed beside a biplane.

Harvey Firestone and his four polo-playing sons by the field. Three are in camel hair overcoats, one in his riding coat and jodhpurs. All are in riding boots.

Mrs. Harvey Firestone in a fur-cuffed and -collared coat in a horse-drawn surrey.

Texas "Hello Sucker" Guinan of New York nightclub fame in Miami for an engagement. She poses by the train tracks in an exotic-looking black taffeta wrap coat with ruffles at the hem, collar, and elbow, with lots of beads and black stockings.

Will Rogers and Joe Smoot at the racetrack, January 24, 1926. Will at the King Cole Hotel swinging a lasso over a group of Beach kids. Will with Gene Sarazen.

Eddie Cantor leaning against the running board of a shiny black sedan outside the Nautilus Hotel.

THE BIG BLOW

. . . practically no danger from summer storms.
—1921 newspaper advertisement for Miami Beach

There was so much building activity going on in Miami that the Florida East Coast railroad couldn't handle the amount of freight coming onto its lines and put an embargo on the shipment of everything but food, livestock, people, and fuel. The shipping lines soon joined the rail embargo. Development was struck another blow when an old, reconditioned sailing ship tipped over in the Miami harbor in January 1926, blocking the entrance for twenty-five days. While 45 million feet of lumber lay in the water, trapping a flotilla of boats, many projects were abandoned.

Land sales steadily decreased as the months passed, but there was still some hope that the boom could stabilize. Then, on September 17, a 125-mile-an-hour hurricane from the Caribbean hit Miami and the Beach in the middle of the night, battering the two cities for hours. In the morning the sun shone and the air became calm, and unsuspecting settlers ventured out to inspect the damage. They didn't know that the eye of the hurricane was passing over, and when the storm hit again from the other direction, many were knocked down or killed by flying timber. The hurricane was considered the greatest natural disaster since the San Francisco earthquake and fire: one hundred and thirteen people were killed in the storm, hundreds more injured, and thousands of homes, many of them flimsily constructed by boomtime developers, were destroyed. Some interpreted the hurricane disaster as divine punishment for the extravagant prosperity Florida had enjoyed.

OPPOSITE: *The 1926 hurricane, inland Miami Beach.*

Ocean Drive, around Third Street, the day after the 1926 hurricane.

TWO EYEWITNESS ACCOUNTS

A Miami lawyer who lived in a Beach hotel described the scene to *The New York Times*. On the Friday before the storm he drove home just before midnight. The wind was fresh, but not violent yet, and there was no rain. Later a strong wind blew out of the northeast; by 3 a.m., the rain came hard, and the sea began to rise, made worse by an incoming tide and the wind, "which whipt the waters into a foaming rage." The door of the hotel was only 300 feet from the high-water mark, but the rising breakers soon crossed the beach to lap at the threshold. Finally one giant wave "battered down the door and rushed through the lobby, leaving it three feet deep in water." Wave after wave followed, increasing the height of the water—

All night long the breakers roared. Hysterical women in the hotel huddled together in little groups on the upper floors, expecting at any moment to be carried out to sea in the hotel.

In order to quiet them we got a man to play the piano and a lot of us began to sing.

About 3 a.m. the wind was raging, and it began tearing the roof from the hotel in huge fragments that whistled weirdly through the air.

Dawn came, and save for the nearness of the other houses, the scene was like one from a ship at sea. Huge combers as high as the hotel came rolling in.

They would crash upon the beach with a force that shook the whole structure, and, seething with foam, break about the building and go hurrying westward toward Biscayne Bay.

The Life and Times of Miami Beach

"I was in the 1926 hurricane, on the 18th of September," remembered longtime Miami Beach resident Olive Delahunt. In the twenties, she and her husband, William, ran Billie's Lunch on lower Ocean Drive, serving up twenty-five-cent bowls of "Coney Island" clam chowder. Along with Wheelan's Fish Grill, Mickey McGee's, the hot dog and chili con carne stands, and the open-air dance pavilions, they were especially busy that night, she said.

So many people came over—nobody knew what a hurricane was, anyway we didn't hear much about them in those days. So instead of people going away from the Beach, people came from Miami to see the waves, they were so high. I did so much business, I couldn't keep up with it. Finally the police came and ordered everyone off the beach and told them to take shelter. I scrubbed up my place, I swept it, I cleaned it late at night. I had a lantern, and we took it and went down to Trotter's place to watch the people dance, that was recreation after working all day. Then they cleaned that out and made us go home. We knew then that it was a bad storm. So we went home to our apartment at the St. David Court. Ohhh, and all through the night the wind was blowing terrible. I think it was one of the worst storms we ever had. They couldn't register the wind velocity. So I sat up all night. The windows blew out and everything was a mess. So when daylight came I looked out the window, everything was covered with water. The ocean came in and met the bay. I saw trees going and houses and everything. So when the water subsided, we decided to go out. I put on a bathing suit and we went down to see how our business was. Well we didn't get that far when everybody yelled, watch out, it's coming back—we went out during the lull. We stood alongside of a building there and it got worse and worse. The rain was just like hail. There was a little garage, with about 12 or 14 people in it, so we went in there, but then we saw the roof going up and down on top of us, so we formed a human chain and went into the Leonard Hotel and stayed there all night. Carl Fisher, I understand, sent down chicken and food

Beach pioneer Olive Delahunt posed in the wreckage of Billie's Lunch, the Ocean Drive café owned by her and her husband.

for the people; the children were the only ones that could have milk. So I immediately went over to help dispense the food—it was at Smith's Casino that they served the food. On Biscayne Street. Of course, we lost our business in that, and many other people did too. We were without lights for a while and water was rationed. Lucky the big town water tank was full of water, so we went down there with jugs and bottles.

Despite the city's attempts to downplay the hurricane's damage, the area's reputation was blemished. Combined with the bad press the city had been getting, the boom met the boomerang. Just as Carl Fisher feared, many buyers of Miami Beach land defaulted on their contracts as their second, third, or fourth payments became due. Tourists shunned the Beach in 1927, and though business picked up again in 1928 and 1929, with the stock market crash in the fall of that year it couldn't recoup.

At the height of the boom, with his assets and equities valued at $50 to $100 million, Carl Fisher had become inspired with a new plan—to build another seaside resort at Montauk, on the eastern tip of Long Island: "Miami Beach in the winter, Montauk in the summer" was his slogan. He bought over 9,000 acres for $2.5 million and committed $8 million more to the construction of a resort hotel, office building, yacht club, and other improvements before putting property on the market. But Montauk was not "a natural," as Fisher once described Miami Beach. Investors were skeptical of its ability to compete with all the other resort towns and real-estate developments—largely inspired by the Florida boom—that had sprung up on Long Island, and Fisher was forced to borrow on his Miami Beach property to help finance the project. Just as the resort was being completed, the stock market crashed, and his already strained finances brought Montauk to a halt. Within a few years Fisher was ruined, and his vitality and optimism were sapped by alcoholism.

Theodore Dreiser felt that Florida—"however vulgarly and stupidly and ignorantly it is being handled now"—had a future that wouldn't die with the end of the boom:

What between the Jesse James real estaters and the patio and thé dansant boys, they have had the thing about all in. And yet I, for one, still think it will go, and go big, eventually. And I will tell you why.

The state is actually within thirty to thirty-six hours of sixty million people, most of whom would enjoy a few days of sunshine and flowers between January and April first. . . . Those beautiful skies. Those perfect days—truly perfect at times—shell-like, dream-like.

Florida did go big—eventually. Unfortunately, it didn't happen in time for Dreiser to make any money on the lots he had bought.

THE BATHING SUIT CITY

The following undated (probably 1927) and uncredited editorial, found in some Miami Beach archives, was a sly spoof on the city's publicity madness.

Miami Beach should set a precedent in dress and become known throughout the world as "the bathing suit city."

Businessmen should go to their offices in bathing suits and robes. That is a very, very sensible idea.

The natural therapy that makes Miami Beach the most healthful playground city in the world is a combination of sunshine and ocean waters. We seem to appreciate this all too little. The wearing of bathing suits to work would create the proper measure of appreciation. The wearing of bathing suits throughout the day would add many years to the lives of those who accept this idea at face value. There are three things that should cause the idea to be favorably accepted: health, convenience and economy.

The other day we walked into the office of William Burbridge, millionaire realty operator. He has a very palatial office in his building at Fifth Street and Washington Avenue. Mr. Burbridge was garbed in a bathing suit and a robe. He was working hard on the details of a realty deal.

Miami Beach is a very unique city. It has many things that other cities do not have. The uniqueness should be added to and capitalized. When bathing suits become the accepted garb of the work-a-day, Miami Beach will become known throughout the world as "the bathing suit city." That will be very fine advertising—very unique advertising.

Digging Out from the Bust: The Thirties

The best thing about Miami is the sea outside and the sky above. Both these are done in perfect taste and as yet the gangsters have not even scratched the surface. Miami is vulgar, noisy, ugly and frantic and you and I can certainly have more fun there than in any spot in all the world.

—Heywood Broun,
Vanity Fair, February 1936

MIAMI BEACH *is calling You*

The early thirties was a time of adjustment. The Depression had shaken everybody up. Carl Fisher, deprived of his nineteen Packards and driving an old Essex that was lent to him by a local businessman, had moved out of his big North Bay Road showcase home with the observation tower. Although he had lost his co-ownership of the Miami Beach Improvement Company, the Pancoasts offered him a job there on salary, and he applied himself to the task of reviving the city's reputation. To his secretary/new wife/frequent drinking partner, Margaret, he dictated letters to all his high-rolling friends of the twenties—*Dear Rube; Dear Will: Why don't you come down here?*—offering them free room and board at the Flamingo or the Nautilus, the posh pleasure palaces of the twenties that were looking more like white elephants every day. The response was less than encouraging. "I have had ten replies from people," Carl wrote a friend, "who, would you believe it, ask for train fare too!" In 1933, J. H. Wendler, editor of the Miami Beach *Times*, published a record-length list of delinquent taxpayers. Just as Fisher had feared, an enormous number of boomtime property buyers had defaulted on their payments.

With Florida banks "popping like firecrackers on a Chinese New Year," according to the Chicago *Tribune*, developers went bankrupt. Construction halted throughout the city. Across the causeway in downtown Miami, wind blew through the girders of unfinished skyscrapers along the bayfront. Dozens of unfinished subdivisions laid out during the boom made parts of the city look like ghost towns, with elaborate gateways, sidewalks, and street signs marking off blank acres of land, and with hibiscus bushes blooming at the entrances to houses that had never been built. Locals pointed out the "Hen Hotel" to visitors, an abandoned shell of a building in Hialeah turned into a chicken hatchery.

The one advantage, if it could be called that, to the collapse of Miami's real-estate boom was that local officials were already veterans of "basement economics" as the national Depression deepened. When the Roosevelt administration created savings and loan associations to help stimulate building, eager delegates from Miami and Miami Beach spent the night on the steps of the Federal Reserve Building in Washington and received, respectively, the first and second licenses ever issued to operate these businesses.

Meanwhile, the city press office valiantly churned out releases heralding Miami's recovery. One slow news day in 1932, readers of *The Daily Alaska Empire* must have warmed up to a report that N. B. T. Roney and the management of the Biltmore Hotel in Coral Gables had joined forces, operating a fleet of "aerocars"—touring buses painted with scenes of local attractions—between the two hotels, so guests could share their golf course and beachfront. Hotel guests were also eligible to take a special train from New York that featured a swimming pool and gymnasium, moving picture shows, and an orchestra. The city came up with catchy new slogans designed to capture the tourist dollar: "Stay through May" and "Bring your trunks empty."

But far surpassing all these polite publicity gimmicks in effectiveness was the Beach's aggressive exploitation of what had in the twenties been a limited amount of "resort" gambling. The city was not alone in this tack: gambling was a huge national trend that swept the country in the thirties, "manifested in illegal gambling casinos, racetrack betting, in card-playing for money, the proliferation of slot machines, pinball machines, punchboard, jar games, bingo, the Irish Sweepstakes, even chain letters," according to a 1936 Chicago *Tribune* series investigating the gambling industry. Soon after the revenue-desperate Florida state legislature passed a law in 1931 legalizing pari-mutuel betting, Joseph Widener, "Philadelphia capitalist and sportsman," remodeled the old Jockey Club and turned it into the Hialeah Racecourse, replete with a new grandstand and an enormous landscaped track with a wading pool and a flock of pink flamingos. Hialeah was such an immediate success that the tourist season became unofficially defined by its racing dates, January 1 to March 15. People soon remarked that Hialeah was to Miami what the Metropolitan Opera was to New York.

The success of Hialeah inspired other gaming ventures, and Miami quickly became a gambler's paradise, at least from late November to late March. After the season ended, local law enforcers allowed the reformists to close them down. By 1936, according to the Chicago *Tribune*, the area offered more gambling than any other place in the nation. Two other tracks, Tropical Park and Gulfstream, were licensed to run at either end of the Hialeah season, and slot machines were legalized in 1935. Their numbers were supposed to be limited by population, but in fact they were distributed indiscriminately, in bars, at the Elks Club, in hotel lobbies, even on the street; when it was discovered that schoolchildren were losing their lunch money on them, the law was revoked. Local law-enforcement officials looked the other way when roulette wheels and black-

The tote board at the Hialeah Racecourse, 1939. Gambling was the primary diversion of the Florida tourist of the thirties. Photograph by Marion Post Wolcott.

jack tables sprang up in nightclubs during the tourist season. Most Miamians agreed that what was good for tourism was good for the city. Payoffs, of course, also made gambling lucrative for local officials. When one honest Dade County sheriff claimed he had turned down $240,000 in bribes in his first two months in office, he was deemed incompetent and forced out of office.

Prudence and perseverance, combined with a liberal assist from gambling, eventually brought Miami and the Beach through the Depression. Even though the boomtime land-sales bubble had burst, Miami was able to maintain its popularity as a resort and a place to live. The turning point in the city's economic recovery depended on something new: the growth of a new budget-conscious tourist market catering to middle- and working-class groups who inspired a wave of new construction. By 1933, while much of the country was suffering its worst year, the Beach was well on its way to recovery and looking forward to another type of boom.

"BLUEBLOOD" MIAMI BEACH

. . . its atmosphere gay, carefree, and expensive.
—*The WPA Guide to Florida*

Most people who have seen the Beach grow up over the decades agree that despite the Depression, and in some ways because of it, the Beach was at its best in the thirties, before the tourist explosion that came after the war. "Better than the twenties?" said Olive Delahunt. "Better than now even." "It was *fan*-tastic," said Stan Platkin, who moved there as a boy in 1939.

June Cutting, Delahunt's sister, vividly remembered her arrival on the Beach as a young girl just as the decade was about to begin. "We were picked up at the train station in an open touring car. I can remember the excitement of driving over the causeway with nothing but water on both sides, glorious gorgeous breezes blowing on me, beautiful moon up above. I said to myself, 'I will *never* leave this place again.' And here I am.

"Personally I think that after World War One, you had the fast life, it was the flapper age—it wasn't an easy time to live," explained Cutting. "But when Prohibition was lifted, the nightlife flourished, the music was great, and people could go out and have fun. I call the thirties the Age of Romance. Young people today just don't know how wonderful it was. You were dressed in a lovely chiffon or organdy gown, had a beautiful life of dancing and dining. Romance was here. All the big bands came here. Business here was great. It was an age of design and romance."

It was during the thirties, after the rough edges had come off the boomtime development and before the city turned into a middle-class tourist mecca, that parts of Miami Beach had an air of wealth and stateliness similar to Palm Beach, the high-gloss neighbor that it was inevitably influenced by and unfavorably compared to, despite the protests of loyal, and somewhat defensive, Beachites. ("What God Had Left Over When He Created Palm Beach" was the subhead for a 1936 *Fortune* profile of the city that enraged the Beach's old guard.) Eventually it would become clear that Miami Beach was not a pale imitation of Palm Beach but had its own identity as a vividly colorful pleasure city for the middle class.

"Miami Beach's streets are definitely smart, as smart as Palm Beach's streets," declared *Fortune*. "There you will find the sleek motors, the clumps of willowy women in frail evening gowns, that are the unmistakable insignia of Manhattan, Boston, Philadelphia." (They might have borne the insignia of those places, but they were probably acquired in the Midwest.) By the mid-thirties, an estimated six hundred millionaires spent the winter season—January through April—in Miami Beach, "more obscure and not so obscure millionaires to the square inch . . . than in any other resort in the country," according to a 1940 article in the Palm Beach *Daily News*. "And that includes Palm Beach, too. But Palm Beach has the glitter

Prospective tourists with money received this brochure; those without received a brochure with a plain paper cover.

names, names that dot the society columns in the big Manhattan columns. Whereas your average Miami Beach millionaire, although he may be hot stuff in his own home town, is sometimes a total stranger as far as the rotogravure pages are concerned."

A 1936 Chicago *Tribune* article noted that millionaires "are a dime a dozen. No one dresses up to visit them. Bankers appear in the shopping district in shorts."

In addition to the motor-industry contingent that Carl Fisher attracted—Harvey Firestone of Firestone Tires; the four Fisher brothers, who built car bodies; vacuum tank inventor Webb Jay; Henry Ford's associate Charles E. Sorensen; Charles Kettering, General Motors' research head and inventor of the self-starter; speedboat manufacturer Gar Wood; and many more—Miami Beach drew the cream of the crop of northern manufacturers. Though their family names may not have shown up among Mrs. Astor's list of four hundred, they brought nods of recognition from American consumers. Even today, as sightseeing boats circle the Beach's nicer waterfront homes, tour guides recite the roster of their former residents: Elmer Maytag, washing machine king; thermostat inventor Mark Honeywell; shoe man Leonard Florsheim; vacuum cleaner maker William Hoover; dimestore-chain owner Sebastian Kresge; automobile rental king John Hertz; Warren Wright, of Calumet baking powder and Calumet horse-farm fame; Life Savers manufacturer Edward J. Noble. Of course, some of the older-money set did choose Miami Beach over Palm Beach. Januarys, the William Kissam Vanderbilts sailed down from Tuxedo Park on their yacht *Ara* to his "palatial" (most overworked adjective of the day) estate on Fisher Island. John Jacob Astor, Jr., made a home on Pine Tree Drive, an ordinary-guy multimillionaire—in the eyes of Miami Beachers—who remained a lifelong bachelor, for many years exciting the hearts of would-be Mrs. Astors among vacationing stenographers. Decidedly unordinary was Colonel E. H. R. Green, son of Hetty Green, the first woman to make a fortune independently on the New York Stock Exchange

and a notorious miser. His mother's money financed a secluded Spanish-style estate on Star Island that Green shared with his sister. Green also lavished some of his mother's money on a Mississippi showboat that he moored behind the house, which could seat four hundred for performances of the Broadway shows Green arranged to have staged there. Dressed in white linens and a panama hat, and accompanied by Stella, his jewel-collared bull terrier, Colonel Green was often seen being driven around the Beach in the glass-roofed, extra-wide car that he had had custom-made to accommodate his enormous girth and wooden leg, the result of a childhood accident. Around the holidays, this peculiar sedan might be spotted in front of Saks Fifth Avenue on Lincoln Road, sale]adies parading out to the open car door to display little girls' frocks for him, a few hundred dollars' worth to be shipped to selected orphanages.

So that even though a non-Beach socialite might say, "Why, there is no society in Miami Beach! Only people who couldn't make it in Palm Beach went there," Miami Beach did have its own version of society. Like everything else about the Beach then and for many years to come, it was just more *nouveau*, more eclectic and freewheeling.

Estates inspired by French châteaux, Spanish haciendas, or English manors were filling in empty plots on the private, man-made islands—Star, Palm, and the three Sunset Islands. They lined prestigious North Bay Road, where Carl Fisher had built a big showcase home for himself during the fat years, and lovely Pine Tree Drive—so named for the row of Australian pines that John Collins had planted to shield his avocado groves from the wind—that wound along beside Indian Creek. Ten and fifteen years had passed since Carl Fisher's two Japanese gardeners had worked their magic on the barren landfill. The trees and shrubbery they culled from all over the world had exploded under the subtropical sun and rain. Framed by heavy palm fronds, shaded by magnificent banyan trees, adorned with trellises straining beneath bright flowering vines

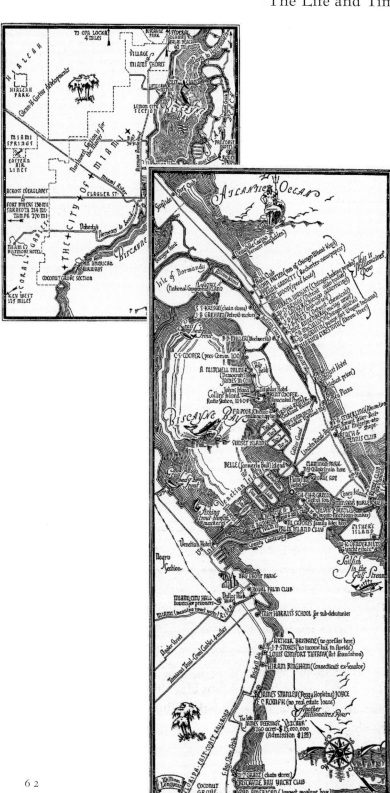

From a 1936 Fortune *article on Miami and Miami Beach detailing the houses and watering holes of the rich.*

of bougainvillea and allamanda, even modest homes acquired a luxurious air.

Damon Runyon, who adopted Miami Beach as his wintertime home in the thirties, lovingly described in one 1936 column what "getting sand in your shoes" means:

It means white and pink houses, with red and blue, and green-tiled roofs, and purple bougainvillea, and scarlet hibiscus crawling over garden walls, and roses, and gardenias, and gladiolas growing in green yards.

It means palm trees whispering mysteriously, and tall mellalucas nodding their plumed heads to every breeze, and birds singing in the quiet mornings.

The inhabitants of this Miami Beach were clubmen and clubwomen, terms rarely used in these postsociety days. In Miami Beach there were, and still are, plenty of clubs to choose from. The richest and most elite was the Committee of One Hundred, a.k.a. the Lonesome Millionaires Club, organized to help restore morale to the city after the 1926 hurricane. "A combination of the Racquet Club, the Rotary Club and the Union League Club," *Fortune* described it. With a few exceptions, members' permanent residences had to be more than 150 miles from Miami Beach. This gentlemen-only club (their wives were busy arranging charity functions and volunteer programs at the Miami Beach Women's Club) met once a week to discuss current affairs and listen to edifying lectures. A favorite topic was "How I Made My First Million." Rowdy behavior was reserved for the annual stag party held at the Cocolobo Cay fishing club, thirty miles south, where, after racing down in yachts, a couple of hundred very rich and reputedly refined men picnicked on hot dogs, popcorn, lemonade, and coconut ice-cream cones, while being entertained by a program of "amusing" events, including a greased-pole contest performed by a group of boys who had probably been imported from Miami's Colored Town for the occasion.

Many of these same men and their wives were members of the Bath Club, a cabana and social club cloistered behind a high wall far—at that time—from the madding crowd at Sixty-seventh Street and Collins Avenue. The Bath Club, formed in the twenties as a refuge for the "better" residents of the city from what was seen as the boomtime flotsam, had an older and snootier membership than its upstart spinoff, the Surf Club, established by publisher James Cox when the Bath refused to admit his friend Alfred Ochs, a Jew. Despite its beginnings, the Surf did not turn out to be much more socially enlightened than the Bath, but it was more in tune with the innate personality of Miami Beach. While the Bath Club sponsored sedate formal dinner dances, the Surf's social director, Alfred Barton, a former set designer for Cecil B. DeMille, staged a series of elaborate theme parties during the season: "Anchors Aweigh" night, for example, had a sixty-foot replica of the *Queen Mary* and a typical dock scene at the end of the club's pool, illuminated anchors and replicas of sailors around the patio, and "underwater settings" featured in the lounge. A St. Moritz night brought five tiers of ice-capped mountains to the tropical patio, with the palm trees wrapped in layers of white fabric, and snow-covered pine boughs lining the walls of the dining room. On Inferno night, skulls were hung from the ceiling, and chunks of steaming dry ice surrounded the red-lighted floor. The Surf also staged Prize Fight Dinners in the thirties, with boxers duking it out in a ring set up in the middle of the din-

ing room. "During the Depression," said Barton, "you could hire a fighter for five dollars a round—some punks for less."

Afternoons dripped lazily by at one's beach club, gossiping with one's equals, or even taking an occasional dip in the sea. There were endless luncheons and bridge games and musicales and balls, as well as occasional evenings mixing it up with the Beach's new café society at the local nightclubs and gambling casinos. News of the city's visitors, down from Chicago or Pittsburgh or Cleveland or Baltimore or North Carolina, but rarely from anyplace west of St. Louis, was likely to show up in the *Society Pictorial*, the local magazine that chronicled Beach society's comings and goings, the size of their yachts, the flowers in their centerpieces, and the party games they played. Here's one entry from the 1929 season.

When Mr. John D. Hertz decides to change his place of abode for a few months, he has quite an extensive bit of moving to do. Most of us toss this and that into a few suitcases or trunks and set sail, step on the gas or climb aboard the train and let it go at that. Mr. Hertz is different.

When he arrived at Miami Beach this week to occupy his beautiful home on 4901 Collins Avenue with Mrs. Hertz and their daughter, Miss Helen Betty Hertz, he had to also see that his 12 thoroughbred horses were safely headed for the Miami Jockey Club stables, that his 15 fine polo ponies were on their way to the Miami Beach polo barns and that his new Sikorsky amphibian airplane . . . was consigned for Miami Beach. . . . Mr. Hertz is already planning some extensive air cruises this winter with Miami Beach as his base. . . . While polo will occupy much of his time when the propellers of his airplane are at rest, he will also be interested, with Mrs. Hertz, in the winter race meeting at the Miami Jockey Club.

The public center of swank was Lincoln Road, where "the ladies in the white shoes and the white hats and the white gloves," as one Beachite described them, strolled down the street's pale pink sidewalks (an inner one for window shop-

Lunch at the Surf Club, 1940. Photograph by Marion Post Wolcott.

Surf Club attendants, 1932.

Members of the Artists and Writers Club at a private dinner at the Beach and Tennis Club, a gambling casino, 1936.

ping, an outer one for circulation). Lincoln Road is "getting busier daily," the *Society Pictorial*'s roving reporter reported, ". . . there's a chauffeur in a big blue car turning on the auto's radio and having a private concert . . . while Milord and Milady are shopping." Sleek façades of native keystone, a kind of limestone, or marble or chromium, were marked only by the discreet signage of stores that also had Fifth Avenue addresses, such as Saks, Milgrim's, and Peck and Peck, fulfilling Carl Fisher's dream for it as the Fifth Avenue of the South. Gift shops sold "tiny nosegays of semi-precious stones, French telephone pads, unusual cigarette boxes," and at the Antique Dome, visitors ogled a jeweled stickpin formerly owned by Edward, then Prince of Wales, while Greenleaf & Crosby jewelers displayed the Miami souvenir deluxe, a diamond-and-enamel sailfish brooch. Behind the big plate glass windows of the Exotic Gardens, petals occasionally fell from huge bouquets of roses. Weary shoppers could take in a matinee at the Colony movie theater, which served tea and cakes on the balcony between shows.

Making a purchase on Lincoln Road was reserved for the wealthy; for everyone else, a trip there was a special occasion, and a child wore gloves and party shoes. June Cutting recalled all her excitement as she accompanied "Jacques the baker" on a Christmas shopping trip down Lincoln Road when she was sixteen.

The stores we had then! In Greenleaf & Crosby you sat on satin couches in the middle of the room and were served tea or coffee or champagne and out they'd come with a piece of jewelry displayed on black velvet. They'd show you each piece one by one. And at Srael and Jabaly, Mrs. Jabaly would say, "Is your wife a blond or a redhead or black-haired?" And they'd send a similar model out. That to me was the technique of good selling. The people dressed exquisitely and they had such magnificent manners that you just didn't know how to say no. Jacques went home loaded with bundles. I remember telling my sister, "Oh, what a wonderful day I had!" Now I could use the caption, "It was like a day in the life of the rich and famous."

The image of a resort full of willowy young women in mousseline de soie evening gowns, streets lined with sleek black

The Srael & Jabaly dress store on Lincoln Road.

sedans, and fine homes decorated by Maryland matrons was the one that the city liked to promote. But in reality the "blue-bloods" shared their paradise now with the parvenues, "the café society," says one pioneer—show people, sports figures, newspapermen, and a growing contingent of gangsters. Even less publicized was the fact that a large number of Jews, once considered among the least desirable of citizens, were establishing themselves south of Lincoln Road, and would swiftly make Miami Beach their town altogether.

The old guard and their successors continued to maintain a lifestyle separate from mainstream Miami Beach, but the city was creating a new elite that would make them obsolete. "The social life of Miami Beach was just whipped cream on top of the cake," Alfred Barton was quoted as saying in Polly Redford's *The Billion Dollar Sandbar*. "Because the real Miami Beach, as I look back on it now over the years, was certainly the theatrical, gangster, middle-class New York–Chicago people who really occupied and made it. They made the hotels and they created an atmosphere here which certainly was quite different from any other town in Florida."

THE SUNNY ITALY OF THE NEW WORLD

A promotional booklet of Miami Beach real estate published in 1932 called "Sun-Sea-Ara" mapped out the city's most expensive neighborhoods and listed the names and occupations of each homeowner. But it studiously omitted the one resident whose name was a household word and whose home was listed as one of the three must-see attractions in the WPA guide for 1939: Public Enemy Number One, Alphonse Capone.

Capone first came down to Miami in the late twenties, rented a suite of rooms at the Ponce de Leon Hotel, and went on fishing trips out in Biscayne Bay. One season he leased a furnished bungalow on Miami Beach, and when the unsuspecting owner found out who her subtenant, "Al Brown," really was, she anxiously expected to find the place in a shambles. Much to her relief, she found everything in order on her return. A few days later, a woman showed up on her doorstep, introduced herself in a soft voice as Mrs. Capone, and pressed a generous check on the woman to pay for an outstanding

Al Capone himself was rarely in residence at his Palm Island home—he went to prison in 1930 for possession of a concealed weapon and was not out long when he was sent back, in 1932, for tax evasion. When he returned to Miami Beach in 1940, he was in the terminal stages of syphilis and suffered from dementia. Every day he would be wheeled out to the water's edge—and quickly retrieved when the tour boats passed by. He ventured outside his compound only on rare occasions, including an appearance at St. Patrick's Church on Miami Beach for his son's marriage. (Years later, Sonny Capone changed his name after being convicted of shoplifting, became a dockworker, and was never heard from again.) During Capone's deathwatch, Milt Sosin was among the flock of reporters camped outside his home. When the word came, they all rushed to call in their stories from the one telephone booth on the causeway. James Cox, the publisher of the Miami *News*, said okay, publish it, but I don't want that SOB's story on my front page.

Despite his limited exposure on the Beach, a little Capone goes a long way, and almost everyone who lived there then had a detail to add to the Capone legend. "My mother said she used to visit my uncle at his house across the street from Capone's. A dozen cars might pull up at his house all at once, then take off all at once twenty minutes later." Or, "I was a delivery boy for Western Union, so I saw a little action. If I delivered a telegram to Capone's house, I'd ring the bell and a little door in the big wooden gate would open and a hand would come out to take the telegram and give me a quarter." Alice Rogers and her friends would be picked up by Jake Guzik, Capone's financial adviser, and his son "in a great big Stutz, with a big dog sitting in the front seat," and they would be driven over to Capone's estate to swim in the pool and fish from the dock. "We'd be served hors d'oeuvres and sandwiches, wined and dined. Scared? I wasn't scared—didn't even think about it."

Harvey Bell was a singer who came to Miami from Pittsburgh in 1930 to work as one of the backup singers for Eddie Cantor's show at the Fleetwood, and never went back on the road. "I sang light opera, big numbers, Mario Lanza. *'Give my looooove to you,'*" he warbled. "None of this 'do-do-doodle and da-da-da dah stuff,'" he said scornfully, belting out a forties melody and snapping his fingers. Bell was singing at a club called Aubrey's Lagoon in the thirties. "I'd see a little girl out in the audience, and she would always listen to me. One day the owner introduced me to her, and she said my dad is Capone's bookkeeper. She was Guzik's daughter. She said, 'Come to dinner Sunday night [at Capone's], we want you to sing.' Well, when Capone says sing, one had better sing. So I drove up, knocked at the big thick doors at the gate. Inside there were long tables full of people. I was just like this"—he mimicked himself shaking—"thought I was going to be shot." (Eddie Cantor had a similar story, of being invited to Capone's house and nervously rushing over to the piano. "If you knew Susie like I knew . . . ," he began to sing. "Hey," said Capone, "I didn't invite you over here to entertain. I just wanted to meet you.")

Although they are innocuous stories, the tellers were often wary about repeating them, as if, fifty years later, the law or the Mafia would make them sorry they ever opened their yappers. "Skip it!" an old lady shouted when her friend mentioned that Sonny Capone was in her class at St. Patrick's school.

Al Capone (right) with his personal trainer at his Palm Island home, 1939.

Capone's Palm Island estate, 1931.

phone bill for calls to Chicago and for any small damages to the place.

At a time when other tourists were staying away in droves, Capone was a most enthusiastic promoter of the city. He praised Miami in a newspaper interview as "the sunny Italy of the New World." "I am going to build or buy a home here and I believe many of my friends will also join me," he declared magnanimously. "Furthermore, if am permitted, I will open a restaurant, and if I am invited, I will join the Rotary Club."

In the depressed real-estate market, he didn't have much trouble finding a house to buy, a medium-luxurious Spanish-style estate on Palm Island built by brewer Clarence Busch in 1922. Homeowner Capone improved the property with a boathouse and dock for his thirty-two-foot cabin cruiser, a swimming pool that could use both fresh- and saltwater, a boxing ring where he took instruction from a personal trainer, and a gatehouse near the heavy-walled entrance that served as a lookout. The master bedroom had a view of the pool and bay, and every night the master laid himself down to sleep in a four-poster with a wooden chest full of cash at his feet—in his opinion, the only safe place to keep money. But he didn't exactly find the rest—"which I think I deserve"—that had brought him to Miami. The governor felt Florida had enough problems without being known as the home of America's number-one criminal, and he ordered Capone's home raided on the grounds that the man was a public nuisance.

Carl Fisher showed up at the hearings that followed, braving Capone's ugly glare to testify that the criminal's presence depressed property values and frightened the good people of the community. Although Fisher himself had buried stashes of liquor in his backyard during Prohibition and never turned down a friendly card game, he opposed organized gambling at the resort. But Fisher got little support from nervous neighbors, and it was difficult to prove that Capone was truly unwelcome in the community, since he had already ingratiated himself by making large charitable donations, and, even more effective on Miami Beach, by throwing extravagant parties.

The most important soirée of the 1929 season was a party Capone threw at his Palm Island home the night before the St. Valentine's Day Massacre in Chicago. Doormen frisked the hundred guests, including local politicians, gangsters, gamblers, celebrities, and a gaggle of sportswriters in town to cover the heavily promoted Sharkey-Stribling prizefight on Miami Beach. It was probably the invitation of a lifetime for most of the guests. Capone led the gentlemen on a tour of his wine cellar and living quarters while henchmen wearing pistol holsters served champagne and canapés. "Capone hires nothing but gentlemen," one of his thugs testified. "They must be well-dressed at all times; they must have cultured accents; they must always say 'Yes, sir' and 'No, sir' when he addresses them." On another occasion, Capone was host to the mayor of Miami, whose haberdashery he patronized—especially after the owners threw in a free walking stick with one particularly large purchase, the first time, the amazed gangster said, that he'd ever been given something for free. Mayor Sewell once attended one of Capone's afternoon "teas," where poker games were played with $1,000 bills. Capone proudly introduced Sewell to Jake "Greasy Thumb" Guzik, "the father of the Syndicate"; Sewell remembered the incident because it was the first time he had ever heard the word "syndicate."

As a result of the mob activity Capone put in motion, that innocence would quickly pass. Capone swiftly introduced the underworld to the pleasures and opportunities of South Florida, especially its laissez-faire attitude toward gambling. In short order Capone acquired a quarter interest in the tony Palm Island Club; muscled in on the Fleetwood's Hangar Room, where he installed two Chicago gunmen; and obtained a controlling interest in the Villa Venice, a bathing-turned-gambling-casino on the beach at Fourteenth Street, as well as in a Miami dog track. The popular Deauville Casino, in the Deauville Hotel at Sixty-third Street, kept him out only by bringing in its own protection from New York.

Guzik, Tony Accardo, and Frank "The Enforcer" Nitti helped Capone run his local operations, but although people said the "muscle" in Miami came from Chicago, in fact it came from New York, according to the Chicago *Tribune*'s investigation. Lucky Luciano, "Long" Zwillman, from the Jersey Shore, New York slot machine czar Frank Costello, and racketeer Frank Erickson, an investor in Tropical Park racetrack, were among the leaders of the Miami mob. Meyer Lansky, Dutch Schulz, and gang members from various other cities also wintered in Miami Beach and began to carve out their own niches of criminal activity.

Miami Beach's "climatological advantages are equally attractive to respectable people and undesirable characters who come here from all the metropolitan areas of the nation . . . to ply their illicit trades," explained city manager Claude Renshaw in a 1936 speech. Once the mob had taken root, it was impossible to weed out. By the time Senator Estes Kefauver came to Miami in 1950 as part of his nationwide investigation of interstate organized crime, fifty-two illegal gambling casinos were operating in neighboring Broward County alone, and gangsters had infiltrated hotels, real estate, and the construction industry.

CAFÉ SOCIETY

Not at all unrelated to the gangster presence—in those days of horseracing, illegal casino gambling, and the entertainment that gambling paid for—was the city's popularity with the "'mob' from Hollywood and Broadway," as *Time* magazine then dubbed it. This was the wintertime watering ground for East Coast café society, a social group that writer Agnes Rogers once defined as "one part wealth, one part fashion, two parts celebrity, two parts night-club press-agentry and gossip-column exploitation," a description that fit Beach tourists perfectly.

Most notable personage among them: Damon Runyon, the syndicated newspaper columnist who captured his gangster

The Life and Times of Miami Beach

LEGS AND LEGS AND LEGS
... unbustled and white, shod and unshod: these are the "girlies" that give Florida its best publicity during the winter season when other U.S. beaches are chill and inhospitable.

STEVE HANNAGAN
As Miami Beach's press agent, he invented the cunning stunts that keep Florida in the rotogravures and newsreels winter-long.

in 1920 had left one of his shoulders mis-shapen. And after a ball struck him on one of his own tennis courts in 1925, he lost the sight of an eye. But he found himself in 1926 with $6,000,000 in cash, $20,000,000 in quick assets, and no debts. His investments in Miami Beach were valued at nearly $25,-000,000. And then Carl Fisher made the one misstep that undid all his work. In the spring of that year, as the last tremors of the boom died away, he made up his mind

to build a summer resort in the North that would carry on for his rich clients where Miami Beach left off in April. The spot that he chose was Montauk Point, at the eastern tip of Long Island, New York.

Now, Montauk Point in summer as often as not is foggy, chill, and inhospitable—as far removed as possible from the warmth and languor of Miami Beach. But un-touched sites for sea resorts are rare in the

North, and a sea resort Carl Fisher would have. So he bought 10,000 acres at Montauk Point and built on them a hotel, polo grounds, a swimming pool, a golf course. Altogether, they cost him around $12,000,-000. Rather than cash in his assets, he mort-gaged his properties at Miami Beach to
[Continued on page 92]

SHE LEAPT FOR A CAMERA

HER MOTHER WEPT
... when this young lady in oranges made papers throughout the land.

SHE GOT FOUR OFFERS

· 45 ·

LEFT: *"Miami Beach," they said, "was built on legs." Thousands of photo-graphs of pretty schoolgirls were sent weekly to news-papers across the country. Carl Fisher's publicity impresario, Steve Hanna-gan, at center.*

RIGHT: *Damon Runyon with his wife, Patrice, who is wearing a horse-and-jockey pin (to the left of her cross). They migrated south every winter with their friends, who were sportswriters and gamblers.*

buddies' life and peculiar language in humorous short stories. Every winter he and his second wife, Patrice, forsook Man-hattan for their home on Hibiscus Island, not far from the house of his friend Al Capone. Las Mellalucas was all white, Patrice's favorite color, right down to Runyon's white type-writer. Runyon had no problem finding material for his columns in Miami, there being no shortage of characters, thor-oughbreds, or show people.

During lulls in the sporting life, Runyon wrote affection-ately about the small-town virtues beneath the Beach's big-city affectations. One column told the story of a world premiere—"the first showing of a picture anywhere except about ninety times in Hollywood, Cal."—at the Lincoln Theater on Lin-coln Road. "Mr. Sonny Shephard, the manager of the Lincoln theater . . . has his dinner jacket newly pressed for a big open-

ing and the pretty girl in the ticket wicket gets a fresh hair-do, and the genial doorman, who always tips you off quietly when to save your money on a picture by holding his nose, assumes a manner of gravity and importance." One of the stars of the movie was supposed to make an appearance, so everyone turned out for the event in their best bib and tucker. But the star turned out to be bandleader Ben Bernie, "who is not a movie star in Dade County, at all, but just one of the neigh-bors. He is the same as Mr. Sailing Baruch, or Mr. Bill Dwyer, or Mr. Jorge Sanchez. You send over to Mr. Bernie's house to borrow a cup of sugar.

" 'Good evening, ladies and gentlemen,' said Mr. Bernie.

" 'Oh, hello, Ben,' came a mild response from all parts of the house. If the greeting lacked anything in spontaneous enthusiasm it was only because we had all just left Mr. Bernie

Digging Out from the Bust: The Thirties

LEFT: *Walter Winchell with his daughter in the Roney Plaza gardens, 1930. Winchell was a wintertime fixture at the Roney until the 1960s.*

RIGHT: *Sophie Tucker and Eddie Cantor, 1934.*

BELOW: *Helen Morgan, famous piano-top crooner, on the boardwalk, 1932.*

his signature greeting, "Good evening, Mr. and Mrs. America and all the ships at sea." Despite his millions of fans, Winchell is remembered by old Beachites as a "rather cold" man who always carried a golf club with him as protection against his enemies.

At various times, a slew of other journalists who moved with their crowd showed up on the Beach. Why, "the writer's colony alone has New York depleted!" brayed the society pictorial gossip columnist. "There are Nunnally Johnson, Ring Lardner, George Ade, Grantland Rice, Laurence Stallings, Damon Runyon, Joseph Hergesheimer, Ray Long . . . and Octavus Roy Cohen's on the way!" Heywood Broun came down to gamble and wrote about it for *The Nation* and *Vanity Fair*, and radio commentator Gabriel Heatter and family settled there. His daughter Maida, author of several cookbooks, owned a two-table restaurant in Miami Beach in the sixties.

Eddie Cantor and George Jessel performed on Miami Beach, the former showing up at the latter's show one night at the Palm Island Club to give an impromptu performance. Comedian Joe Lewis appeared at the Roman Pools Cafe. Tom Mix, at the same, demonstrated that he could play every instrument in the orchestra, which he managed to do in a rendition of "Pony Boy." Sophie Tucker seems to have been everywhere. Irene Bordoni, French singing star, performed at a benefit for the homeless in Flamingo Park on Miami Beach. Helen Morgan, for whom the expression "torch singer" was coined, performed at her friend Mother Kelly's bar and at the Beach and Tennis Club, the swankiest gambling establishment in town. A highly bronzed Al Jolson spent many hours sunning himself by the Roney Plaza pool. Photographers dogged the heels of composer Irving Berlin, and coaxed a bashful smile out of him when he took his pale and skinny body to the beach. (While most other men by that time were wearing trunks only, Berlin, like Damon Runyon, modestly wore a top as well—Runyon suggested in one column that men in one-piece bathsuits should be escorted to a bathhouse and forced to examine their chests in a three-way mirror). Miami's Pan

at the race track a few hours ago and would see him again a little later at the Royal Palm."

Walter Winchell, gossip columnist and radio broadcaster, had no trouble getting the Roney Plaza management to give him a suite of rooms every winter in exchange for his priceless promotion of the hotel. In Winchellese it became the Rooney Pleasure in his local weekly broadcasts, begun, as always, with

The Café de la Paix was located on the beachfront side-walk that ran between the Roney and the Traymore hotels.

OPPOSITE: *Entrance to the Roney Plaza Hotel, 1939. Photograph by Marion Post Wolcott.*

Poolside at the Roney, 1939. Photograph by Marion Post Wolcott.

OPPOSITE: *A record day of 75,000 bathers, 1937.*

American air base was a favorite place for photographers to catch visiting celebrities. When Charles Lindbergh, handsome and "slim as a finger," as Runyon wrote, came to inspect the Pan Am operation, photographers clicked away as he tried out the cockpit of a clipper seaplane. Eleanor Roosevelt, who spent a vacation with friends on Miami Beach, was shown being greeted by the mayor of Miami as she emerged from one.

Unofficial headquarters for café society—as well as for prosperous middle-aged businessmen and their wives, assorted gigolos, "dolls," and gamblers on a roll—was the big pink ("garish," said *Time*) Roney Plaza, with its double-height Spanish archways and huge tropical gardens enclosed within its L-shaped mass. Women in light sundresses or white sharkskin trousers, turbans, and sunglasses, the men in tropical-weight suits, came out to have lunch beneath the big polka-dot umbrellaed tables at the Roney's Café de la Paix. Days were comfortably whiled away at one of the $300-a-season cabanas equipped with dressing rooms, showers, and lounge chairs,

which surrounded the swimming pool or faced the sea along a boardwalk decorated with gay Venetian poles and wrought-iron lanterns. Lunch or tea would be served to guests beneath the canvas awning of a cabana by white-jacketed stewards pushing carts piled with silver, glasses, and covered dishes. The "cabana vogue" spawned special cabana accessories, such as tile-topped cabana tables equipped with "gay canapé sets," while ladies dressed in "cabana pajamas," according to a fashion report.

Somewhat more exertion was required for a day at the race-track, the main attraction in Miami, drawing eight to ten thousand people every day. The track broke down into three social classes: a palm-lined drive to the clubhouse was reserved for horseowners and the chic set; the grandstands were filled with the broad middle range of tourists; and the fifty-cent bleacher seats went to "jaunty Negroes and overalled whites [who] may watch to see which horse and jockey look the luckiest," according to a 1935 *New York Times* article. The remarkable thing about Hialeah, about Miami overall, the *Times* noted, was how little it felt like the rest of the nation. "The man with the showy suit and the big cigar, the poker face and the feeling in his bones that tomorrow he will be a millionaire again, is the key character in Miami. In Miami, it doesn't seem to be 1935 . . . the time is 1929 and the attitude is 1929—taut and carefree simultaneously."

Evenings were devoted to the casinos and nightclubs, usually an establishment that combined the two. The swankiest was the Beach and Tennis Club, whose name was inspired by Palm Beach's renowned and equally unathletic Bath and Tennis Club. It was a place of "sparkling glass and bright silver, and soft footed waiters, and gleaming shoulders, and white shirt fronts, and gentle music," as Runyon described it. This elegant establishment was owned primarily by gambler Mert Wertheimer. It was housed in what had once been the Shadows, the home Carl Fisher had shared with his wife, Jane, on the beach at Fourteenth Street. A roulette wheel now turned in the same place Fisher once slept beneath pictures of his heroes, Lincoln and Napoleon.

A close second to the Bath and Tennis in elegance was the Brook Club, in Surfside. The Brook's longtime doorman would, in the sixties, remember Miami Beach in the thirties as a place where there were only two chinchilla coats in town and everyone arrived at the club in a chauffeured limousine— "Now it's the other way around." The Palm Island Club was owned by New York bootlegger Big Bill Dwyer, who also had a stake in Tropical Park. His casino tended to be raided more often than the others because, the Chicago *Tribune* reporter surmised, "the boys" felt that he was already pulling in his fair share at the track. Broadway showman Earl Carroll ran the nightclub there, putting on $15,000-a-week shows that featured "36 of the most beautiful girls in the world." Carroll relinquished his concession to Papa Bouche, who staged semi-

nude "French" reviews (the kind of entertainment a generation of Beach kids, out with their parents, grew up on). The Villa Venice—"gangster headquarters," noted one magazine map—was another popular gambling spot, though somewhat less chic. And the Deauville Casino had an "exquisitely chummy room," according to Heywood Broun.

Down at the southern tip of the island were the two Carter casinos, run by George Carter, the owner of a pier at the foot of First Street. Backed by Tommy McGinty, the gambling boss of Cleveland, the two places did the most business in town, said the *Tribune*, "and although some swankier competitors called them sawdust joints, they would be pretty snooty places in any other surroundings." Each had fifteen roulette wheels working, seven or eight craps tables, blackjack, chemin de fer, baccarat, wheels of fortune, and faro. Although most of the roulette games had only a 50-cent minimum in chips, it wasn't unusual for heavy gamblers to play $5,000 to $15,000 a night. "Sand in your shoes," wrote Runyon, meant "Carter's, with the elbowing, excited crowds around the dice games and the roulette wheels, and the insistent voice calling 'make room for players, men.'"

Some thought that the Beach's entertainment scene was too sophisticated. By the mid-thirties, some local business leaders, "many of whom wore the hood and robe on meeting nights," enlisted the Ku Klux Klan to put pressure on places that featured striptease acts and high-stakes gambling, as well as "private clubs where anything goes," which probably meant places that featured female impersonators. But trying to curb perceived immorality was probably only part of the motivation. More likely the raids were instigated by Miamians who may not have been sharing the profits from gaming and entertainment and were jealous of the Beach's success. When the Klan wrecked the La Paloma Club in 1937, *The New York Times* reported that the organization represented citizens who wanted the city "less dependent on winter tourism and more year-round." In response to the Klan's threats, the popular French Casino nightclub turned into a movie theater, and the

Palm Island Club, the Club Ha-Ha, and half a dozen other places closed. What the Klan wanted in Miami they got. After wrecking the La Paloma, Klansmen dared the Dade County sheriff to make a reprisal; the sheriff did one better and issued a statement supporting the raid.

SOUTH BEACH SOCIETY

Meanwhile, south of the fancy homes of the better-mousetrap manufacturers, and south of the sybarites at the Roney, swanky Lincoln Road marked the border to another Miami Beach—bustling South Beach. Colorful small hotels lined up across from the broad public beach, whose sands were covered with a happily cabanaless crowd. Block after block was filled with chunky little apartment buildings, and delis and fish stores and cafeterias and souvenir shops thrived on Washington Avenue. But if the style of South Beach was different, so was the substance—a large proportion of the tourists and residents were Jewish, a remarkable situation in light of the times.

Many Jews were drawn to Miami and the Beach in the tide of people swept in during the boom years. Some of these newcomers stayed despite the animosity they encountered then—the local manifestations of a wave of anti-Semitism that began to sweep the country in the twenties. Carl Fisher's groundbreaking slogan had been twisted on a popular bumper sticker to read, "It's Jew'n in Miami." Members of the newly revived Ku Klux Klan, which had added to its hate list Jews, Catholics, new immigrants, and those opposing Prohibition, staged marches down Flagler Street in the mid-twenties. Less overt but more significant to the city's development was the clause that Fisher and his colleagues inserted in deeds that prohibited the sale of the land to Hebrews or "Syrians." The term "Syrian" indicated people of Arab or Middle Eastern descent, thus excluding all Semites. It was then a standard real-estate practice. Jews, it was generally assumed, were simply not good for business, a point of view that was relatively new in this country.

The beginning of social discrimination against Jews could be traced back to a nationally publicized incident in 1877. Joseph Seligman, a Jew and one of the most prominent bankers in the country, was turned away from the Grand Union Hotel in Saratoga Springs, New York. Seligman was head of the most important brokerage house on Wall Street and had been the key figure in raising bonds for the Union government during the Civil War. After the war he was asked by his friend Ulysses S. Grant to become the Secretary of the Treasury, a post Seligman turned down. Despite the fact that Seligman had been a guest at the hotel for several years, the owner of the Grand Union—who may have been trying to even an old score against him—had issued an order not to allow "Israelites" to patronize the hotel. A highly publicized debate flared up afterward, and gave a voice to incipient anti-Semitism around the country. Other resort owners announced their intention to bar Jews from their establishments, and gradually the belief that it was good policy to keep out Jews spread to include real-estate developments, clubs, and other private institutions. In Miami Beach, Jews were not only prevented from buying land and homes, they were barred from playing golf at the private courses and from joining the social clubs like the Bath and the Surf, and discouraged from registering at the prestigious Fisher hotels, the Collins family's Pancoast Hotel, and most of the other "better" hotels.

Still, it wasn't easy to regulate such a large, popular resort; making sure that Miami Beach would never become a "Jewish outfit" took some planning. Inventing discreet ways to welcome Fisher's Jewish friends, as well as "high-class Hebrews," while excluding the general run of Jews, inspired a rash of memos between Fisher, his hotel managers, and other interested parties on the Beach. Fisher, for example, advised a fellow hotelman not to enclose a card with his hotel brochure that said, "Hebrew Patronage Is Not Solicited." "You can usually tell by the names of the people applying for apartments and their occupation whether they are desirable or not," wrote Fisher. The manager of one hotel, to which Fisher had sent a Jewish friend, relayed his thoughts on the "problem": "It is very well and good if we welcome Mr. Sam Rauh, who is an upstanding fellow, but then he will send his friend, Mr. Charley Rauh, and Mrs. Rauh, and their three children." Fisher saved another letter written to him by a visitor during the twenties who found himself the victim of this discrimination double standard.

Mr. Carl Fisher:

Enclosed find clipping which speaks for itself. Mr. John Hertz is a Jew, I don't believe he denies it. Evidently you are the type of man who has a prejudice against the Jew if [he. is not rich] enough. Christ, who was a friend of the poor and lowly and not the rich, could not buy at your end of Miami Beach, nor would he be allowed to play golf, because he was a poor Jew. I [, who] employ about two hundred Christians and have always been considered by them a friend, was denied the privilege of playing golf on your links because I did not deny I was a Jew. . . . This was my first trip to Miami Beach and my first experience in that form of prejudice. A bit out of date don't you think—simply not of a true Christian spirit. Your Glenn Adams told me he was sorry. I told him that I would not care to play where Jesus Christ, St. Paul and St. John would not be allowed to play because they were Jews.

Regretfully Yours
Harry Klein
c/o Klein's
Peoria, Ill.

The cavalier anti-Semitism of the twenties is revealed in a spoof written for Carl Fisher by Leo Carillo, a popular entertainer of the time. "Second Payment Blues" was to be sung to the tune of an Irving Berlin song, "What'll I Do?"

The opening night of the season at the Hotel Leonard, 54 Ocean Drive.

What'll I do?
It can't be true my second payment's due—
What'll I do?
I know a guy
that I could sell it to,
but he's a Jew—
What'll I do?

It was a different story in the Lummus development in South Beach. Perhaps twenty Jewish families were living on Miami Beach by 1922, most of them in South Beach—until the boom years, except for a few isolated estates, that was virtually the only place anyone could live on Miami Beach, and for many years it continued to be the only area with groceries and other business services. By 1926, the Jewish population of South Beach had grown enough to support a synagogue, Temple Beth Jacob, located on Fifth Street. As Polly Red-

ford explained in *The Billion Dollar Sandbar*, the Lummuses were from Georgia, where small communities of Jews, some dating back several generations, existed in many towns. Devout Christian southerners not only tolerated Jews but they often revered them as the chosen people of the Old Testament. However, while the Lummuses knew no tradition of excluding Jews, they did limit the sale of land to Caucasians.

Jews who came down to Miami discovered that they had privileges in South Beach not available to them elsewhere in the city, perhaps even more than they were accustomed to in their hometown. Binder boys looking to make a buck off the boom, soldiers who passed through on their way to the Spanish-American war, trombonists in a traveling orchestra, those who came on doctor's orders—an extraordinary number of the histories of local residents begin with a mother with severe allergies or an asthmatic little brother seeking relief in the warm climate—discovered a small but flourishing Jewish community on the Beach. Many Jews were inspired to return and settle there. Surely South Beach was more inviting than Chicago or New York during the winter, and anyone with a little vision and some daring could see that the developing resort offered great opportunities. A Chicago milliner named Katie Pollack, for example, came down in the mid-twenties and started a business dynasty for her twelve children and their families. She began with a South Beach parking lot, made enough to lease one South Beach apartment building, then another, then enlisted her sons in building hotels and apartment-hotels, one after another, working their way up the Beach as the city expanded. The extent of the family's business and success may have been unusual but the system of building, buying, selling, trading upward, was a familiar pattern on the developing Beach. "They couldn't lose, they couldn't lose," said Audrey Corwin Wright, Pollack's granddaughter.

Few resorts in the country were open to Jews, either as hotel owners or as tourists, and the ones that were, summer resort areas like the Catskills, Atlantic City, and other New Jersey sea-side resorts, had become virtual holiday ghettos. Many Jewish hotel operators from up north found a perfect opportunity in Miami Beach to make their business year-round, and they took advantage of the stricken real-estate market to buy, build, or lease hotels and apartment buildings. The Levensons of Tamarack Lodge, the Weiners of White Roe Lake Hotel, the Muravchicks of Kenmore Lake House, the Grossingers, the Rosenthals, and the Jacobs family were among the Catskill or Jersey Shore contingent that established hotels in South Beach. Gradually their summertime clientele followed them down. "At the 10th Street Beach you'd meet all of Sullivan and Ulster counties," David Levenson remembered.

The growing popularity of Miami Beach with Jewish tourists is reflected in the *Jewish Daily Forward* newspaper ads of the thirties. In 1935, only the Nash Hotel at Collins Avenue and Eleventh Street, owned by Morris Nashelsky, and the Victor Hotel, on the Beach at Twelfth Street, advertised. But in 1939 the page for hotel advertisements was loaded with Miami Beach locations: the Nemo, the Hotel Astor, Goldberg's Seymour Hotel, Luber's London Arms, the Nassau Hotel, Bernstein's Harrison Hotel, the President Hotel, the Hotel Helene, the Hotel An-Nell, Hotel Evans, the Ritter and New LaFlora hotels. Even the management of the Fleetwood, formerly restricted, now found it worth their while to advertise in the *Forward*, and in Yiddish, too.

A number of these new tourists "got sand in their shoes," and further swelled the Jewish population. Although exact numbers are difficult to determine given the floating, seasonal nature of the population, Jews made up approximately 20 to 25 percent of the Beach's population by the late thirties, and their number tripled—from 6,494 in 1930 to 28,012 in 1940. Thumbing through copies from the late twenties of the *Seminole*, the Ida Fisher High School yearbook, only a few Jewish family names stand out—Cassel, Weiss, Fleeman, Glickman—but they predominate in a yearbook from 1933. Their power was being felt in the city. Malvina Weiss Liebman Gutschmidt remembered when "there was a big effort to elect a Jew to the city council, who was Baron de Hirsch Meyer, in 1934. It wasn't many years before the Jewish commissioners had to make an effort to elect a gentile to the council."

Most Jewish families lived south of Lincoln Road, but some lived in the middle and upper Beach areas. Although these neighborhoods were supposed to be restricted, there were problems enforcing the covenants in deeds after the property had changed hands. "As for oceanfront estates," Polly Redford noted in *The Billion Dollar Sandbar*, "most of the Beach agreed it was better to have them filled with Jewish millionaires than no millionaires at all, and raised no objections when movie moguls Albert Warner (Warner Brothers) and Nicholas Schenck (Metro-Goldwyn-Mayer) bought castles by the sea."

How does an ethnic neighborhood grow? In the case of Miami Beach's Jewish community, one native described it simply and well.

I think the discrimination was a big factor. In the early days there were signs on hotels and apartment homes that said No Jews Allowed. Many of these older Jewish people were in business in New York and were wealthy. They wanted to enjoy the sun, too, and the beauty of this area. Imagine you come down at this season, and they hear there's no room at the inn. They thought, what is this? And it is a terrible thing, to be plagued with this. *They wanted to enjoy a life here in the wintertime.* They worked hard all year, they felt they deserved this kind of vacation, this was close by plane or train—New York to Miami was a direct link. So they said, look, we want to partake of this place too. Then after there was a stock market crash, after things got difficult here, they came in and said, Hey look, now we're going to invest. That's our best way of saying we belong here. So, with real Jewish ingenuity and business acumen, they came in, and this is when you started to see the surge of the hotels being built. When the Jewish people come in to a community naturally they want to set up things they like. There's got to be bakers that make good rye bread and pumpernickle and danish. So therefore there's room for a Jewish bakery, and for delicatessens and fish stores. Then other stores come, like clothes. All the merchants begin to come little by little. Eventually, Washington Avenue was lined with wonderful stores.

But anti-Semitism grew in proportion to the number of Jewish tourists, residents, and businesses. It became standard for gentile-owned hotels and apartment houses to openly advertise their restrictive policy in brochures and ads, or, more blatantly, on signs over doorways or beside the buzzer. "Restricted clientele," "carefully selected clientele," "gentile owned and operated," "restricted patronage," or even "*definitely* restricted clientele" were the usual variations on the theme—all these terms were used in ads placed in the Miami Beach Hotel and Apartment book for the 1937–1938 season, issued by the Miami Beach Chamber of Commerce. Jewish hotel owners had their own code phrases, such as "dietary laws strictly observed."

Those were the "nice" ways to put it. One hotel adopted "Every room with a view but never a Jew" as its slogan, and many people remember signs that read, "No Jews, No Dogs." Irma Rosenblatt saw one when her family moved to the Beach in 1939. She was eleven. "I'd never heard of anti-Semitism before—I'd never heard anyone say there was anything wrong with being a Jew. But then one day I saw a sign on the lawn of one hotel that said 'No Jews or Dogs.' That really scared me. I thought 'Oh no, there must really be something bad about being Jewish!' "

The people who were safe from the signs remember their role reluctantly. One gentile woman admitted that she was given an apartment building as a wedding present "and would you believe it, we put up a sign that said No Jews. No, let's see, that's not how it was worded. Oh, yes—Restricted Clientele. I hate to admit it," she said, shaking her head. "It's a terrible blight on your record. But we did it. I was so young, I didn't question it. Everybody did it. I even remember once we had a guest come in from the Bahamas, a Mr. Kahn, I think, very successful guy. And I asked him. Asked him if he was Jewish, just like that. He denied it, but we always thought he was. Can you believe it? Argghh, it makes me want to run into the closet and hide."

"In those days, segregation was adamant and you had to be this way about Jews, which certainly cost us a lot because we missed a lot of very good people," said Kay Pancoast, whose in-laws owned the restricted Pancoast Hotel. "There was a lot of feeling, which is too bad, but I think it's about gone. I don't really come in contact with that a'tall anymore. We're getting better about black people, but we still have a long way to go."

This unusual phenomenon of a booming Jewish resort shoulder to shoulder with a swanky restricted one did not go unnoticed by observers. *Time* did a feature on Miami Beach's amazing success in 1940, noting that "swarming thousands of thrifty folks stretch a year's savings over two weeks in South Beach, where there are many small relatively cheap ($5–$7) hotels, the dog-track, drug-store lunch counters, the only

Ocean Drive, looking north from Ninth Street, at the end of the thirties building boom. To the right is Lummus Park.

public beach space. Collectively they bring millions in cash to Miami Beach. Their tide is spreading northward to and past 15th Street, where (at Alton Road), an apartment hotel is a symbolic outpost. The sign: GENTILES."

The *North American Review* ran an essay whose writer, Padraic Colum, makes his own sympathies clear in these not-so-subtle descriptions of the Beach:

The pelicans are not the only curious creatures on the beach. Massed in thousands are human beings whose legs, stomachs, bosoms, hips and heads are as unbelievable as are the beaks, wings, neck-pouches of the contiguous fowl. I suppose that in everyday garb each and every one of them would pass . . . for not too violent divergencies from the human norm. But with wrappers and singlets for covers, with large masses of nudity showing, they do not seem as if they belonged to any ethnic group we know of. . . .

There are beaches and beaches here. And as one goes to where the gatherings are less dense the human type becomes increasingly recognizable. On one carefully guarded beach I behold young women whose costumes are enchanting and whose figures might go on a frieze, and young men who are worthy to go beside them. They are, of course, the rich and the high-born.

ANOTHER BUILDING BOOM

To the first-time visitor, its shining spires, its tropical foliage, the incredible blue of its waters, the cloud formations that tower in the background—all sharply etched under an intense, white sunlight—appear as ephemeral as a motion-picture set.

—1939 *WPA Guide to Miami*

As tourism grew, the city enjoyed a wave of expansion that increased each year until the war temporarily halted it. Between 1930 and 1940, builders put up 2,028 homes, 164 hotels, and 485 apartment buildings. Despite the modest size of Miami Beach, by 1940 it ranked fourteenth among all the cities in the U.S. in the number of building permits issued. Much of this construction was going on in the undeveloped land south of Lincoln Road.

Throughout the thirties and into the early forties, South Beach bloomed. Hotels went up along Collins and Ocean Drive, apartment buildings filled the blocks west, and new stores, theaters, bars, and nightclubs went up on and around Collins and Washington avenues and Lincoln Road. Just in the first six months of 1938, twenty new hotels and one hundred apartment houses went up. "It happened all at once. We went home in May, came back next fall and didn't recognize it," Bea Muravchick remembered.

Most of the new buildings were small, economical in plan, and designed in a local hybrid of the modern styles popular during the Depression. The architects of South Beach used a kind of Chinese-menu design technique, picking and choosing among the motifs of the richly decorative Art Deco style seen in Europe in the twenties, and blending them with elements of the streamlined style popularized by American industrial designers of the thirties. The resulting architecture, like much of what was designed in the twenties and thirties, is today generally referred to as Art Deco, a sixties coinage derived from the title of the groundbreaking design show held in Paris in 1925, at which many of these styles were first publicly presented, the Exposition Internationale des Arts Décoratifs et Industriels Modernes. But at the time the sleek new look was simply called Modern—"Moderne" if you knew the lingo, "Ultra Modern" if you were promoting the product, and sometimes, if you happened to be a local architect with some disdain for South Beach, "modernique."

Whatever the label, it was clear that a sea change in style and taste had taken place in the ten years since the height of the boom. The twenties drive for a more cultured and luxurious life looked backward to historic styles of the old world— French, Tudor, and particularly in Miami Beach, the romantic Spanish-Mediterranean style. Although the Spanish style was still very much alive on the Beach in the thirties, especially in private homes, builders of South Beach's hotels, stores, apartment buildings, and small homes seized on the modern as an appealing and practical solution to the Beach's building problems. It was "new," which had an obvious value during the Depression slowdown; it looked neat and cheerful; it was fast and inexpensive to build; it lent itself to colorful decorative touches that heightened the get-away-from-it-all vacation experience; and it bore a moviesque familiarity that guaranteed its popularity.

South Beach's Art Deco buildings were exciting to look at, rich with pattern, texture, color, shadow. Cylinders, cubes, pylons, spheres jutted out of façades, although their function was primarily decorative, a means of jazzing up the buildings' basic boxiness and giving them some distinction from their neighbors. One exception to this functionless trend was the ubiquitous "eyebrows," the little concrete ledges that mushroomed out of the façade over windows and supposedly blocked the sun's glare. The streamlined style, an innovation of industrial designers who had stripped trains, ocean liners, and automobiles of extraneous details and contoured the mass into one sleekly curved, aerodynamic object, was a wildly pop-

The lobby of the Georgian, a typical modest Ocean Drive hotel.

ular and easily adaptable design concept. Its functional origin was forgotten as everything from desk clocks to rest homes was streamlined. In South Beach even the smallest hotels managed to incorporate shallow but dramatically varied planes into the exterior, to include curved corners with wraparound windows, or to emphasize strong vertical or horizontal lines. Although each Beach hotel took pains to look unique, the two hallmarks of hotels from the thirties are a central vertical element that thrusts into the air beyond the roofline, projecting a skyscraper effect, and the use of "racing stripes," bands of color that wrapped around the planes of the façade. "We used to say that if you designed a building and it didn't look like it was going 50 miles an hour, it didn't look like it was in style," said T. Trip Russell, an architect working on the Beach at that time.

Most of the new hotels were two, three, or four stories high, people-sized buildings where even a roofline detail of an undulating wave would not be lost on visitors admiring their bright new hotel from across the street or socializing on the obligatory veranda. Beach architects applied a host of charming small flourishes to the surface of their buildings: a starfish and seaweed scene etched into the plate glass doors or a decorative porthole window; panels of glass block that dazzled in the sun on a façade or created a luminous space in an interior wall; stucco friezes of gladioli, water jets, sunbursts, or lacy leaf patterns picked out in aqua or pink or sea green; a bright aluminum stair railing stylized as a cascade of water; cool terrazzo floors tinted in clear tropical greens and yellows and laid out in modern geometric patterns.

Here was the local, homespun version of the dazzling mod-

The model modern hotel of South
Miami Beach combined elements of
an ocean liner and a high-speed
train, with streamlined corners,
nautical round windows, racing
stripes, and a neon shipstack.

The dining room of the Grand
Plaza, 1937. Murals, tinted terrazzo floors, and plaster bas-relief
panels were typical interior details.

The Albion Hotel, 1939, sailing through the balmy Florida evening.

The lobby of the Albion.

Washington Avenue was the main shopping street for South Beach in the thirties.

ern architecture usually seen only in big-production movies. Except for some new theaters—85 million people were going to the movies each week—and post-Prohibition bars, little else besides movie sets was being built during the Depression. Only here the set decorator's world was shrunk to fit the scale of the Miami Beach hotels and the pocketbooks of their guests: a decorative spire or loopy winged tower did homage to the movies' fantasy skyscrapers; MGM's grand-hotel lobby devolved into a curved marble reception desk, an oval table, and a pair of brushed-aluminum torcheres; the shiny black Vitrolite that reflected phalanxes of Busby Berkley tap dancers trimmed a doorway; and the neon glitter of Broadway was re-created in hundreds of glowing hotel signs. But a trip to Miami Beach was better than stepping into a thirties movie, because the people inhabiting these little hotels weren't debonaire millionaires and fast-talking blondes, they were just nice people like us, and, as one Beach resident's mother used to say, they were "OK"—our kind—not "TK"—their kind. Besides, Miami's

tropical weather, its exotic palm trees and flowers, had a glamour that the movies' big-city settings couldn't equal.

South Beach's modern buildings lost their novelty and charm in the succeeding decades (owners tried to neutralize their dated looks with coats of beige paint). The glamorous movie aura they once exploited had evaporated in an instant; it wasn't many years, 1958, before a movie called *A Hole in the Head* was set in an Art Deco hotel as a way of representing the end of the line for its ne'er-do-well manager, played by Frank Sinatra.

Of course, time passed, and thirties movies, thirties design, and thirties South Beach all came into fashion again. Only in this reincarnation of South Beach, celluloid and concrete have bonded even more thoroughly than the first time around. In the early days of the Deco District, as the South Beach neighborhood is now called, its promoters evoked images of Ginger Rogers and Fred Astaire to describe South Beach in the thirties, even though snapshots of the Beach from the time show a distinctly less glamorous cast of characters. What seemed to be deliberate misinformation was actually creative history-telling. Movies can be mined for certain kinds of information about the past the way some photos or novels can—they capture and communicate the feeling, the mood, of the time they were made, in ways that more conventional sources can't. Movies are an especially appropriate source for a place whose style borrowed so heavily from them, and for a neighborhood whose vast and peculiar architectural uniformity seems like nothing so much as a fabulous, forgotten studio backlot.

"It *was* like a Fred Astaire and Ginger Rogers movie," said June Cutting, trying to mediate the image gap between sylphs in satin dresses and chubbies in $11.80 evening gowns from Klein's. "I think they're speaking of the life-*style*. People *seemed* affluent. They lived with an elegance. The hotels were new, and they all looked beautiful. At night, people walked arm in arm along the ocean. They brought their lovely things so they could look good when they went out to a nightclub or a local restaurant in the evening. At night, it became like a fairyland. People *went*, they were *going*—there was a glamour to them, no doubt about it."

Even people who disdained the tourist life of South Beach were seduced by this urban oasis. Then, as now, the heart of South Beach was the strip of Ocean Drive from Fifth Street to Fourteenth Street. Only the western side of the street was built up. To the east lay palmy Lummus Park, the wide white beach, the jewel-colored sea, and gorgeous cumulus clouds hovering in the tropical sky. "When you sat on one of those porches and you looked across and heard the whooshing of the wind through those palms and saw the water lapping the sand and the glow along the beach, it was effing beautiful," said Audrey Corwin Wright, whose father, Albert Anis, was the architect of many South Beach buildings. "It was the only part of the Beach that really had a kind of grandeur or romance. This had the quality of a little mystic Tahiti or something. It was totally different, like nothing that was going on in New York or Chicago or Pittsburgh."

TOURIST LIFE

Although a trip to Miami Beach became relatively inexpensive in the thirties, it was not a journey to be undertaken lightly. Most people came down for six weeks, two months—never less than a month, in any case. "You didn't fly two hours to see what's doing in Miami," said Mike Mersel, who moved to the Beach after a thirties vacation. "You took the Silver Meteor, it was thirty hours." Three steamship lines stopped in Miami on their way to Havana, but most people preferred the new fast trains, like the Silver Meteor, the Florida Special, or the Champion, several of which left New York for Miami every day.

An article in the travel section of *The New York Times* in 1939 described the rhythm of train travel and the experience of new middle-income tourists. Train departures, it noted, were not unlike ship sailings, attended by friends wishing good-bye, boys delivering messages and gift boxes, drawing rooms filled with flowers. One-way coach to Miami from New York on the Florida Special, for instance, was $22.48 in 1936; a pullman fare went for $41.45. Southern-style dinners were served for 50 cents. A valet and a maid were available, even a barber and manicurist. Some of the new deluxe fliers, or crack trains, were deemed quite "modernistic," as they were popularly described, from their gleaming streamlined stainless-steel exteriors to the easy chairs in the public cars decorated in bright colored leathers and flashing chromium trim. In addition to observation, club, and lounge cars, trains included a recreation car, a kind of "moving night club in miniature," according to the *Times*, where passengers could rhumba or tango to a five-piece orchestra, for some reason known as a "Hawaiian band." Determined vacationers went on dancing all night, long after the purplish night-lights had gone on in the darkened passenger cars, where children in flannel pj's had snuggled into their seats and parents snoozed on rented pillows.

The train hit D.C. at 4:30 p.m., and Richmond, Virginia,

by sundown. Passing through Georgia in the middle of the night, the silhouettes of pine trees and live oaks loaded with Spanish moss were barely visible. The train approached the lights of Savannah at four in the morning, and at dawn it hit the northern Florida flatlands, covered with spruce pine and palmettos. For a while, the train ran alongside the highway, where road signs advertised tourist camps named "Beautyrest" and "Paradise" with come-ons like "Camp Here and Pick Your Own Fruit." Then the train paralleled Indian River, which was in fact a 150-mile-long intercoastal waterway lined with hundreds of groves yielding prized Indian River citrus. The fruit hung bright against dark, glossy leaves, and here and there the train passed tiny white cottages, the typical home of the native Florida "cracker." Cabbage palmettos and avocado groves appeared when the train hit the Atlantic Coast. Passing through the cars, the conductor pointed out eucalyptus trees and recommended the oil from boiled leaves as a cure for mosquito bites. Finally, as the train neared the Gold Coast, the stretch between Palm Beach and Miami, the whole scene changed. The natural terrain was replaced by substantial houses with carefully landscaped gardens, luxurious lawns, and royal palms.

After the train pulled into Miami, visitors took a bus or limo to their hotel or apartment building; car rentals were available, but rare, and since driving down was for the less-affluent tourist, who probably wasn't coming to Miami Beach, there

Every year, Burdine's department store created a special fabric. In 1935, it was inspired by a hit Irving Berlin tune, "Moon Over Miami."

Strolling beach photographers delivered their candid shots to the tourist's hotel. The inscription on the back of the lower photograph reads: "Do you think you can find me, look and try. Sadie."

was no parking problem, despite the dense winter population. (No parking! complain the new residents of the renovated 1930s apartment buildings.) Season-long tourists often rented an efficiency apartment in one of the scores of little two- or three-story apartment houses that filled the blocks of South Beach. Their owners dedicated their new investments to family members, and today a kind of invisible legacy survives in buildings with names like the Don-Bar, the Helen Mar, the Moemil, the Herbshire, and the Hotel Mersel.

The 40-60-80-room hotels on and around Ocean Drive often borrowed names from their grander, big-city counterparts—the Savoy, the Park Central, the Shoreham, the Essex—or took sea-inspired names like the Tides and the Breakwater. Most had lobbies arranged with doily-covered sofas and arm-chairs, area rugs, standing ashtrays, etcetera, all the comforts of the Brooklyn or Bronx apartment their thirties patrons had left behind. The rooms were small, but so what? You didn't stay in your room if you were coming down to Miami! You made a beeline to Washington Avenue, a block west of Ocean Drive, to buy a beach bag and coconut suntan oil, the latest cotton sundress and terry-cloth robe. In mules and a wrapper, you made the trek to the beach each day, blankets and friends crowded together, sharing the Yiddish newspapers and the movie magazines picked up at the newsstands along the way. It was a glorious tropical Rockaway. Lying on the beach, you could watch new hotels going up on Ocean Drive across the street, follow the sightseeing blimps as they floated overhead, and dig for colored shells to bring home, before showering off

Pan Am, the country's first airline, was based in Miami.

at the Tenth Street entrance. Maybe you took a fishing trip on the *Seven Seas* for a dollar a day, or played canasta or bridge on the hotel porch, or got dressed up in white gloves and a hat to visit Lincoln Road, the Rue de la Paix of the South, making a long window-shopping tour from Washington Avenue to Alton Road, then back again.

If you were staying at an efficiency apartment for the season, Washington Avenue was the place to shop for dinner, lined with fish stores, kosher butchers, delicatessens, bakeries, greengrocers, the Piggly Wiggly. Few of the hotels had dining rooms, so if you were staying in a hotel, you probably ate out on Washington Avenue, too, where you could find some of the greatest names in New York and Atlantic City cafeteria and kosher cuisine. Maybe you'd see Al Jolson eating "flannel cakes" (waffles) at Bob Feinstein's Manny's, or some other

celebrity at Winnie's Waffle Shop on Twenty-third and Collins, which stayed open till three or four in the morning for a post-gambling nosh. Holleman's, Hoffman's, the Southern, and the Waldorf cafeterias all did a brisk business catering to thrifty South Beach tourists. Teddy's on Ocean Drive, between Tenth and Eleventh, advertised seven courses for 65 cents "under the tropical sky with the surf at your feet." Without the surf, you could get the same for 50 cents at the Roxy on Twelfth Street. Wheelan's Fish Grill ("Out of the Ocean, Into the Pan") offered fish, salad, roll, and coffee for $1.

In the oldest area of the beach, south of Fifth Street, open-front stores sold souvenirs: shell knickknacks; pecan baskets; assortments of tangerine marmalades and coconut patties; masks made from carved, painted coconut husks; souvenir

The greyhound races, at the southern tip of the Beach, provided budget-minded tourists with the entertainment alternative to Hialeah and the casinos, 1934.

neckties. Up at Burdine's department store on Lincoln Road, you could even buy a piece of clothing cut out of the Moon-Over-Miami fabric the department store had made up the year of that hit tune. Sidewalk stands sold fresh-squeezed orange juice for 10 cents a glass, 35 cents a quart. Bingo parlors and con games lined the street. On Carter's Million-Dollar Pier, you could find dice games and a dance hall and Minsky's burlesque show—also called a "girlesque"—promising "40 Gorgeous Girls direct from Billy Minsky's Republic Theatre on Times Square."

On special nights, dressed in your best bib and tucker—evening clothes were required on Thursday and Saturday nights, but most wore them every night—the casino limousine picked up guests in front of their hotels and whisked them off to Papa Bouche's or one of the other nightclubs for dinner and the floor show, and, of course, admission to the back rooms. Less glamorous but "extremely decorous in spite of the fact that most of the patrons dance in shorts," said the Chicago *Tribune*, was the Oceanic Gardens, east of the Spanish Village, where tourists could gamble and dance to the Kayo Klippers. Of course, the main event of any South Beach evening for decades to come was the dog track at the tip of the island, where just a quarter's admission could buy Hialeah-style excitement.

"Sand in your shoes," wrote Runyon, meant "teeming South Beach, where by day the old men with whiskers and skull caps stroll contentedly in the sun, and their women sit knitting and gossiping on the hotel verandas, and where, at night, there is a steady murmur of voices in the streets, and crowds in the pin-ball establishments, and always, at intervals, the shrill blast of music from the dog track that means that the racing hounds are parading to the post."

Not everyone appreciated the charm of South Beach, however: "Wandered lower end Miami Beach," wrote Meyer Berger in "The Log of a Rolling Motorist" in *The New York Times* in 1937. "Stumbled into vest pocket Coney Island. Same smells, same people, same ballyhoo. Hurried away."

LOCAL LIFE

Living in and creating this developing tourist city, with its aura of fast money and Broadway, were the members of a very small town, who were in the unique position to both enjoy the razzmatazz (in season) and go back home every night. And you didn't have to go out to a chic casino to have a brush with celebrity—any tourist could do that. Living on Miami Beach meant going to school with Knute Rockne's daughter and Al Capone's son and having Ted Lewis stop to help you land a barracuda as you fished in Indian Creek.

By May, though, the big city eased back into its small-town lifestyle. The population dwindled to a few thousand, and, as locals liked to say, you could shoot a cannon down Lincoln Road (or Collins or Washington) and not hit anyone. On hot summer evenings storekeepers on Washington Avenue put picnic tables out on the sidewalk and everyone in town came down to share iced melons—watermelon days, they were called. Kids played in tennis tournaments and diamond ball games or toted their Brownies to their Kodak Club meetings at Flamingo Park, thirty-three acres in the center of South Beach. The park was dedicated in 1930 after a campaign led by community activist Rose Weiss, known as the seventh member of the six-member city council. To protect themselves against swarms of mosquitoes in the summer, people attending the nighttime ball games in the park would cover their skin with citronella oil, wrap their legs in newspapers, and arm themselves with switches of pine. "You'd go 'rah rah,' and swish overhead and 'rah rah' and swish down below," one old-timer demonstrated. A beach party—a party held on the beach!—was a big event. A picnic was prepared—lots of fried chicken, potato salad, and sliced tomatoes wrapped up in packages and kept on ice from the icehouse—and carried to the beach with chairs, balls, and umbrellas. Or sometimes "after

The *Ladies' Home Journal* suggested packing for a four-week excursion to the tropics, 1937:

In a case that went direct:

3 silk suits, black and white, black and yellow, green and white, each with a cool sleeveless dress and unlined jacket or cape

3 evening dresses—piqué, crepe, and one satin or lace, with a jacket

2 cool afternoon dresses, one black marquisette, one navy georgette—for Sunday night suppers and evenings when formal dressing isn't necessary

3 summer sports dresses—white, natural-colored crash, brown with white polka dots

A velvet shoulder cape for breezy evenings

Bathing suits and slippers

3 string berets, white, navy and brown

2 hats—a white panama and a black shade hat

One pair white buckskin pumps

One pair evening sandals

Underwear, handkerchiefs, white cotton gloves and a limited number of accessories, including 2 evening purses, a white daytime bag and a plentiful supply of sun-tan oil

For a traveling bag:

Dark tailored going-away suit

3 blouses, one colored and two white, one of these satin to dress up the suit for social occasions

Dark taffeta evening dress

Simple black dress, "suitable for almost any hour of the day"

Black silk sandals to be worn either afternoon or evening

Necessary changes of underwear (mostly of rayon, which can be rinsed out easily en route)

Toilet articles

Tailored washable silk dressing gown (to double as a beach robe)

some of the fellas went out to get stone crabs, we'd build a wood fire under a washtub to get the water boiling, put tables up on the sand and cover them with newspapers, and we'd boil 'em up, crack 'em, and eat 'em. We'd have a feast of stone crabs. Didn't pay twenty-three dollars for six of them like we do now."

Just going for a drive to see what you could see was terrific entertainment. Sometimes locals went out to find the funny coral castle an immigrant from Latvia was building as a monument to his lost love, or drove to the Pan American Airways terminal in Coconut Grove to watch Clipper seaplanes take off from the water or to study the huge illuminated revolving globe inside the terminal. Or they could take a trip to the Musa Isle Indian village on the Miami River—a tourist adventure in their own town.

Young people went to the Pig Trail Inn on Fifth Street on dates, a drive-in that sometimes had an orchestra on a bandstand, where they'd sit in their car and order barbecue sandwiches and Cokes that they'd mix with a little rum from their personal stash. But if a guy took you up past the Roney, where it was still mostly mangrove jungle, "he was up to no good." In the summer, Ocean Drive experienced a kind of "Jewish spring break," said David Fleeman, whose family moved to the Beach in the early twenties. "There was a network of Jewish families from cities like Montgomery, Atlanta, and Mobile who wanted their sons and daughters to meet. So young Jews from all over the south would come down for a vacation then, and rent rooms for a dollar."

Although the rich and the highborn made a point of avoiding "the other Miami Beach," everyone, from uptown and downtown, came to eat at Joe's Stone Crab down on Biscayne Street. Joe Weiss had been a waiter in New York before coming to Florida for his asthma. He started a sandwich counter at Smith's Casino in 1913, but opened a restaurant as the city prospered. In the early twenties, the lowly stone crab, once native to Biscayne Bay, was brought to his attention, and it was discovered that boiling and chilling them killed their iodine taste. Boiled, chilled, cracked, and iced, the stone crab was such a hit that by the thirties the restaurant was cooking 3,000 pounds of them a day (although only the claws were eaten). Sherman Billingsley, Bernard Gimbel, Gene Tunney—said to have trained on them one season—Runyon, Winchell, Heywood Broun, Jack Dempsey, Al Capone, Jimmy Walker, and J. Edgar Hoover were among the restaurant's regulars.

Joe's, which is still owned and operated by family members, has been one of the consistent landmarks on Miami Beach. In the thirties, it was one of the few things that always looked familiar to winter residents who returned each fall to find that so much had changed.

The High-Rolling Years:

1940–1953

Miami is a rude revelation: I had not really known this was going on.

—Edmund Wilson, *Red, Black, Blond and Olive*

The Beach made such a comeback from the bust and the Depression that *Time* made it one of its 1940 cover stories. A kind of urban miracle had taken place: while other cities were still suffering from the Depression, little Miami Beach saw forty hotels go up in 1940 alone, as well as 313 homes, at what may have been the highest average cost in the country. Miami Beach was "a unique U.S. phenomenon," raved *Time*; one of Miami's "claims to fame is that it is the city near Miami Beach." With better and cheaper transportation, masses of new tourists were flowing into the city. Once they got there, they found that luxury and the aura of celebrity were available to them, too, even if only by association or through a plate-glass window.

A ten-day trip from New York to Miami Beach during the winter season could be had for $137.05 or less, according to a 1940 guide, *101 American Vacations*. The budget breakdown:

Round-trip coach, rail $42.05
(bus, $29.90)
Hotel ($5 per day, 10 days) $50.00
Spend on train for meals $5.00
Tips $5.00
Spend at Miami Beach $25.00
Incidentals, extras, added pleasures $10.00
$137.05

The traveler could take the Seaboard Air Line's Southern States Special or Silver Meteor or the Atlantic Coast Line's Tamiami train. The Southern States Special left Pennsylvania Station at 11:00 a.m. and arrived in Miami at 5:20 p.m. the next day. A hotel on Ocean Drive or Lincoln Road had winter rates of $3.50 to $9 for a double. Golf was $1 day. Locker, towel, and suit rental at the beach was 75 cents to $1. Fishing in a party cost $2 a day, and sight-seeing boats were $1 for two hours. Movies were 60 cents, the dog races were 25 cents, nightclubs usually had no cover charge, and cocktails were 50 cents or less.

For Heavenly Relief from HAY FEVER

Miami Beach

Read the tale of the Pollen Hunters and learn the wonderful truth ————————➤

The big picture magazines brought the story of Miami Beach to the uninitiated. *Life* zeroed in on Lincoln Road, calling it a miniature, rolled-up-in-one version of Fifth Avenue, Michigan Boulevard, Bond Street, and the Rue de la Paix, "the kind of shopping section Hollywood might think up. Down the middle of the wide walks run big plots of grass and a row of palm trees. Rich ladies step sedately out of limousines and sporty ladies hop out of bright roadsters." It was a "world of dream merchandise," a museum of materialism where tourists from Allentown could marvel over pear-shaped diamonds and $10,000 sable coats, see silver reputedly owned by the Hapsburgs, scrutinize a copy of *The Confessions of St. Augustine* that had been underlined by Queen Anne of England, and try on the same dress model at the Jay Thorpe Salon that the Duchess of Windsor had bought the month before. Chic specialty shops like Lilly Daché hats and I. Miller shoes, and the best department stores, like Saks Fifth Avenue and

PHOTO BY MIAMI BEACH NEWS BUREAU

DC-165—Lincoln Road
Exclusive Shopping Center of
Miami Beach, Florida

8B-H736

"Dear Folks, We are here and it is all people say it is. . . . Eve and Herbert." Lincoln Road.

BELOW: Life *staged this exaggerated glamour shot for a 1940 story on the Beach. In the early fifties, one toy manufacturer produced a Miami Beach doll dressed in a mink coat and sunglasses—her hair also grew by a winding device—that sold for $295. Photograph by Alfred Eisenstadt.*

Bonwit Teller, had branches there. (Buyers noted that not-so-chic size 44 was more popular on Miami Beach than in New York.) After business hours, window-shopping tourists promenaded from the ocean end of Lincoln to Alton Road, then back again.

Miami was the marriage and the divorce capital of the country in the early forties, outstripping Reno. Over 10,000 couples were cut free every year in the Dade County courthouse—divorce suits made up four out of every five cases before the six circuit judges. Florida had broad-minded divorce laws, and it took only ninety days to establish residency—and you didn't even need to be there if you found an understanding landlord who'd accept a check for three month's rent. It was a marriage mill, too—a lot of the newly divorced couples went up one flight to apply for a marriage license after getting the decree.

A 1941 movie called *Moon Over Miami* was inspired by the city's luxury-and-love reputation. Two sisters from a small Texas town, on a mission to find wealthy husbands, splurge

their small inheritance on a vacation in Miami Beach, "where rich men are as plentiful as grapefruit and millionaires hang from palm trees," according to heroine Betty Grable. The film shows a montage of real footage taken at the Beach—an aerial shot of its hotels and their gleaming swimming pools along the oceanfront; the old Roman Pools windmill; mansions; boats in the bay; the tower of the giant old Flamingo and a modern neon sign flashing its name. Then the action turns to a movie-set-Moderne bungalow, seemingly at the Flamingo, that the two sisters take with their aunt. The bungalow is a dream, far better designed than anything that actually existed on the Beach: a big, light-filled room, painted a pale, smoky blue with white bas-relief wall decorations, white furniture, and rattan window treatments. The bathroom had a curved, glass brick wall, and there was a private patio behind the bedroom. All the bungalows—all filled with fun-loving young men and women—encircled a terrace with a lovely reflecting pool in the center. Grable, wearing a blue fox-trimmed dress, checks in with an array of matched luggage containing her extravagant new wardrobe. The manager comes to deliver a bottle of champagne from young playboy Bob Cummings, who is having a party across the way; shimmering, flouncy dresses are spread across the furniture to choose from. The young revelers dance—the rhumba, of course—around the patio, and conduct romantic tête-à-têtes in a sunken garden. The only authentic touch was that the pansies in the garden had wilted under the movie lights, as they would have under the Florida sun.

CAMP MIAMI BEACH

The post-Depression celebration of dream merchandise, inanimate or human, was suddenly interrupted. Just as the city was enjoying its biggest year, the United States entered the Second World War. When German submarines were sighted cruising the shipping lanes off Florida's east coast, the Miami Beach publicity department rushed in to help offset "the far-fetched rumors of war hysteria in this area." A memo was sent to staff members suggesting testimonials from visiting celebs: "Miami Beach was never better"—Al Jolson; "A beautiful, peaceful interlude"—Joan Crawford; or even the all-purpose "Two wonderful weeks at Miami Beach and I could grapple with a director," to which staff publicists could attach the name of their choice.

In February 1942, a German U-boat torpedoed the *Pan Massachusetts*, a gasoline-loaded tanker just miles off the coast. That same day, the Army Air Corps announced that it intended to billet and train officer candidates and enlisted men on Miami Beach. Tourists were notified that they had to surrender their rooms within twenty-four hours. Five hundred men showed up overnight to move into five Beach hotels at $10 per man per month. By April, the military had taken over 70,000 rooms in the city—85 percent of the Beach's 332 hotels. The city turned into the most beautiful boot camp in the country.

Most of these teenage boys bunked two and four to a room in the hotels south of Lincoln Road. They had reveille on Ocean Drive, calisthenics on the sand, and took ocean dips four hundred at a time. They attended lectures on the golf course behind Lincoln Road, went to classes among the nude murals at Papa Bouche's, and took their meals at Hoffman's Cafeteria. Locals remember the soldiers best for their marches down the avenues singing "Dinah," "I've Been Working on the Railroad," and "I've Got Sixpence." Even the soldiers unlucky enough to receive their training there in the summertime, when it was so hot that they'd take a shower with their uniforms on, were delighted to find themselves in the subtropical paradise they had only read about. "Dear Mom," one soldier wrote home, "the army sure has gone swell all of a sudden, and it's just like the travel folders say."

If the invasion of a couple hundred thousand U.S. soldiers wasn't enough of a distraction in the community, German and Italian war prisoners were transported daily from a detention

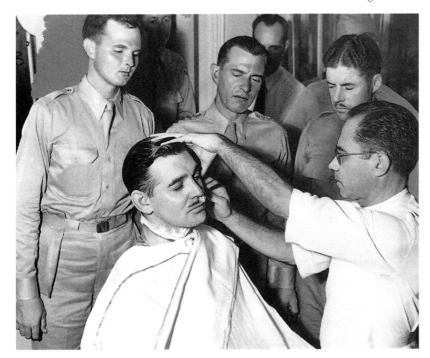

Clark Gable getting the regulation shave and haircut at the Army Air Corps' officers' training school on Miami Beach.

camp in southwest Miami to work details on Miami Beach. Some dug ditches in Flamingo Park, near where the junior high school girls' gym class exercised. "They worked with their shirts off, and some of them were so handsome," Irma Rosenblatt remembered. "I didn't know whether to hate them or swoon over them." A Miami *News* reporter went to get more information about the war prisoners at "women's intelligence headquarters—a beauty salon." One customer told a story about walking behind two old ladies as they passed the military garage where some of them worked. "A prisoner, she said, stepped out of a group and boldly addressed one of the women in a loud voice, in German. 'I didn't know what he said, naturally,' this girl said, 'but the old lady surely did. She began slamming at his head with her purse and answering him in German. I could tell she wasn't calling him any pet names, either.'"

Critics of the city liked to suggest that the occupation of the

The army saved an enormous amount of time and money when it discovered a ready-built encampment named Miami Beach. The shore served as a giant drill field.

Miami Beach was a choice training assignment, especially in winter.

BELOW: *Eighteen-year-old private Robert Armbruster on the steps of his "barracks," the Shepley Hotel.*

hotels was the only thing that would have kept the Beach afloat during such a desperate time. But, in fact, despite gas rationing, tourists continued to pour into the Beach—sometimes packs of young women took the bus down to meet enlisted boys— and competed with the families of enlisted men for space in the apartment houses and in the few hotels not taken over by the military. One nightclub entertainer performed this song about the housing shortage:

Ladies and gentlemen, I came to Miami for a vacation.
But where do I live? At the railroad station!
Now for ten weeks or more
I've knocked on every door,
From every roof to the cellar floor.
And every answer I've had was "NO!
NO, WE HAVE NO APARTMENT—
WE HAVE NO APARTMENT TODAY."
BUT I finally found me a place and all would agree
It's a pleasure, a treasure—it's a HOLE in a tree.
And the landlord, the snooty with a high, nasal squeak,
Demanded "ONE HUNDRED AND FIFTY A WEEK."

To some, it almost seemed unpatriotic for Miami Beach to have taken on such a gala air. "Do We Know There's a War On?" was the name of a 1945 *Look* magazine article that lambasted Miami Beach for harboring "probably the greatest concentration of war-money-to-burn citizenry from every state in the nation." At the same time, the article played up the juicy details of the city's "prodigal luxury and high jinks" for the

reader's delectation, like the case of the visiting executive who spent $859 on a party for eighteen, the cocktail party for 175 that was thrown at Ciro's, a "chi-chi supper club," and the $10 dinner bills and $5 bar tabs civilians routinely rang up, while a GI's budget was $50 a month. *Look* faithfully mentioned the nude floor show at Papa Bouche's La Bohème nightclub, the midnight stripteases, the rhumba madness, and "Miami's current anthem: *Rum and Coca-Cola*." (In fact, the most popular Miami Beach wartime drink was a B-29, concocted from two jiggers of rye, bourbon, or gin; two jiggers of passion fruit; one jigger of pineapple, and one jigger of lime.) Photos illustrated the crowded cabana area of the Roney Plaza, "booked solid since the first of the year," where rates averaged $37 a day for a double room and a cabana rented for $65 a week and up. One shot of a government sign banning pleasure travelers on trains was juxtaposed with a photo of two frowsy-looking women sitting on a crowded beach with cigarettes hanging from their mouths and of men playing high-stakes gin rummy. Some pictures documented the goodies available for purchase in Miami Beach, with captions that listed their going rates: $1,000,000 for a few pieces of jewelry, $40,000 for a Bolivian chinchilla coat, $1,200 for an antique Chinese brocade purse, $2,500 for a bathing suit trimmed in Russian ermine and an ermine-tail-trimmed parasol (this particular suit turned up in publicity shots for years, sometimes priced at $5,000). *Time* in February 1944 declared that "Midas has moved back to Miami": the racetrack at Hialeah was taking in up to $1 million a day, the dog tracks $100,000, and real estate was "changing hands at million-dollar tunes." Men were required to wear ties at Miami nightspots, which were roaring despite a midnight curfew on serving liquor, and if they didn't have one they could rent one for a dollar.

"Sumptuous gambling casinos operate full blast," wrote *Look*. "Black markets are rampaging. Everyone's having a wonderful time.

"A GI Purple-Hearter wonders: 'Is this what I've been fighting for?'"

Look duly pointed out that Miami Beach was housing a quarter of the entire Army Air Corps' personnel during training, and noted the service of the Recreation Pier association—townswomen who volunteered to run Carter's Pier for the soldiers, with dances and meals and a dormitory where GIs on furlough could stay. Merchants gave discounts to servicemen, restaurants furnished them with five hundred free meals a week, and volunteers raised a fund for gifts, free movies, and moonlight rides. Yet *Look* faulted Dade County's community War Chest for collecting less than two thirds of its quota. Above all, "our battle-stained fighting men expect a little self-denial at home—particularly by those who have sacrificed least."

"From the storm of criticism Miami Beach took refuge in the argument that it was a community founded on luxury," wrote *Life* the same year, "that its economy could not function except at high prices."

The fact that a large proportion of the tourists were Jewish made the city even more susceptible to criticism. The leaders of B'nai B'rith sent out a letter to various synagogues suggesting they ask their congregations to restrict tourist travel to Miami Beach during wartime to make room for the servicemen's families. This would eliminate an acute situation, the letter read, "which is now creating contempt throughout the nation."

The army also had to handle "an epidemic of anti-Semitism," wrote Miami historian Helen Muir in *Miami, U.S.A.* The South Beach area, where most of the men were billeted, was predominantly Jewish, and "some of the boys got the idea that only Jews were enjoying wartime vacations at Miami Beach," wrote Muir. "Officials . . . stressed the fact that north of the Roney, where the signs 'Gentiles Only' or 'Restricted' were still hanging in certain small hotels and apartment houses, there were just as many winter visitors."

Although locals protested that everyplace in the country was enjoying a boom, Miami's probably was, as *Life* complained, "out of all proportion." Hotel owners whose buildings were not occupied by the military were making a killing and were busily expanding their empires. Real estate was bought and sold at a furious pace at escalating prices as a wartime ban on new construction met a population increase. After the war, the selling cost of many homes more than doubled, a situation shared by other Florida coastal resorts, many of which were also taken over by branches of the military. In some Florida cities, pieces of property were changing hands three times a year.

The people largely fueling this postwar Florida boom were the men and women who trained there, who had found Florida an unforgettable experience, with its palm trees and flowering bushes, tropical limes and avocados, and, of course, tropical weather. By the end of the decade, as ex-soldiers returned to Florida to settle down with their new families, the state's population increased by more than 80 percent, with Miami Beach leading in growth.

Hordes of wartime tourists made fortunes for the owners of unoccupied hotels, despite calls for "fewer tuxedos and more overalls."

The chorus line at the Latin Quarter.

REALITY CHECK

After the war, hotels had to be repainted and refurnished; plumbing and electrical services needed repairing, and barbed wire along the beach had to be removed. But even if it could be physically restored, the atmosphere of the city had changed completely. The treasured aura of exclusivity that it partly achieved in the thirties was gone. The original moneyed winter residents of Miami Beach, "the blue bloods," from the local point of view, were getting old and their children no longer wanted to come to Miami Beach, either because it wasn't fashionable for their set or because they couldn't keep up their parents' estates. That Miami Beach "died a natural death," said James Wendler, the former editor of the Miami Beach *Times*.

Miami Beach was solidly middle class by this time, and sol-idly Jewish. The population had risen from 28,000 in 1940 to 46,282 in 1950, and by 1947, nearly half the residents were Jewish. When you included the Jewish population of the city of Miami, the numbers exceeded such long-established Jewish communities as St. Louis, Newark, Baltimore, and Pittsburgh. The Beach got a new synagogue, Temple Emanu-El, as the center of the Jewish community moved north. The restrictions on hotels were challenged by a group of local residents after the war. The city sponsored an ordinance, passed by the state in 1949, that made it unlawful to display signs, ads, or notices that discriminated against any person's use of a public place on the basis of race or religion. Some hotels and rental apartments continued to let it be known in their own ways that Jews were not welcome, however. One woman who had helped manage some apartment bungalows next to a private restricted club recounted how she had carefully steered Jewish guests over to chaise lounges on the side of the pool farthest from the club! Certain social clubs, country clubs, and neighborhoods re-

Even after the war, oversized Deco-inspired hotels were filling any remaining gaps on lower Collins Avenue.

The Dubler family's 1948 Passover seder, Miami Beach–style.

As ethnic divisions became more pronounced, so did advertisements of "exclusivity." Some hotels bore bronze plaques stating "Gentiles Only."

mained officially restricted until the seventies, although many Miamians contend that some clubs effectively continue the practice today.

The new ordinance did not significantly change the status of blacks on Miami Beach—which was, in effect, no status. Blacks were not allowed to rent or buy on the Beach. Some worked on the Beach, but they lived in a small area of Miami, which had the highest degree of residential segregation by race of a hundred large American cities in 1940, 1950, and 1960. During the postwar years, its 40,000 blacks, 10 percent of the city's population, were squeezed into less than a quarter square mile of the city's sixteen square miles, most living in one-story shacks, with three to fifteen shacks on a city lot of 50 feet by 150 feet. Their movements in the city were severely restricted. They were not permitted downtown after sundown, not permitted to drive a car below Northwest Fifth Street, not permitted to walk on some Coconut Grove streets without a pass from a local employer.

The same restrictions held for the Beach. If blacks were

coming over to work—for many years, they sat on the "colored" side of the trolley that took them across the causeway—they were required to carry identity cards and to leave the Beach by sundown. Interestingly, the requirement for identity cards and curfews was respected despite the fact that there was no official legislation regarding it, according to former Miami Beach chief of police Rocky Pomerance, who searched the books for such a law when he took office in 1963. Many Beach residents are proud to have secretly "harbored" black live-in help during those years.

The big hotels didn't have many black workers then, although author Zora Neale Hurston was employed as a maid at a Beach hotel in the late fifties. No one knew that her stories had been published in the *Saturday Evening Post* and that she was listed in *Who's Who*. Sometimes, she later explained, you just had to spend time using your hands.

Until the 1964 Civil Rights Act struck down racial segregation laws, welcoming blacks as hotel guests was completely out of the question. The Blackstone Hotel booked a convention for the African Methodist Episcopalian Church in 1954 despite threats from the Klan, but the experiment wasn't repeated. A year earlier the Betsy Ross Hotel manager booked 150 black delegates to a Church of God in Christ Convention—other hotels had booked blacks attending conventions but never so

Although the "better" hotels didn't employ many blacks until the sixties and seventies, Zora Neale Hurston (not pictured here) worked as a maid at a Beach hotel in the late fifties. No one knew that her stories had been published in the Saturday Evening Post *and that she was listed in* Who's Who. *There were periods in life, she later explained, when you just had to spend time using your hands. Photograph by Marion Post Wolcott.*

many at once—but they eventually canceled their reservations after threats of violence against them. The city convention and publicity director hastened to reassure that restrictions wouldn't threaten community *or* business standards in the future. The convention of the National Education Association, which had a firm nonsegregation policy, would go on as planned the next month. Only a handful of blacks was expected at the convention, the director pointed out; they would eat only at their hotels and they would not use any of the city's public facilities or the beaches. In fact, the only beach in Dade County that blacks could use was one on Virginia Key, a then-undeveloped island off the Rickenbacker causeway to Key Biscayne.

Until 1963, when Harry Belafonte was given accommodations at the Eden Roc, even top-name black entertainers performing in Miami Beach hotels and nightclubs couldn't stay on the island; they'd have to go back to Overtown, the black neighborhood northwest of Miami's business district, to stay at the Lord Calvert, Mary Elizabeth, or Sir John hotels. As a result, Overtown became the place for late-night entertainment for locals, both blacks and whites, who'd come over to see performers like Count Basie, Ella Fitzgerald, and Lena Horne put on after-hours shows. A large part of Overtown was razed for the construction of Interstate 95 in the early sixties, displacing thousands and destroying what had been its thriving entertainment district.

Maintaining restrictions was particularly difficult in a place that had such wide appeal and such a taste for celebrities. One retired hotel owner relayed a story that showed how this next generation of hotel owners and city officials "managed" the discrimination policy against blacks, as Jews had once been managed. He recalled getting a call in the mid-fifties from Jackie Robinson, then first baseman for the Dodgers, who was in Miami with friends, including Joe Louis, then heavyweight champion, to play in a baseball/golf tournament in nearby Miami Springs. They wanted to play golf on the Beach's Bayshore Country Club course, but had been told they

couldn't play there unless they were staying in a Beach hotel. Could he say they were registered at his? The hotel owner called the city manager and said, "We have a problem." And the city manager said, "You have a problem." "I said, 'Look,'" said the hotel owner, "'why don't you have a better excuse at the course?'" Finally they agreed to say that since it was high season, the hotel was booked but that they could mention the owner's home address at the golf course, and they would be allowed to play. "So in that way," said the hotel owner, "we avoided a situation."

The legacy of segregation lingers on. Miami, which has had some of the worst race riots in the country, is still near the top of a list of sixty urban areas in black residential segregation. And the black population on Miami Beach didn't register on the census until the eighties.

THE PACKAGED VACATION

Automobiles, airplanes, and air-conditioning—locals say those are the three things that made Miami Beach. With the evolution of Carl Fisher's trailblazing highways into sleek interstate highway systems and the growth of a massive postwar automobile market, nearly three-quarters of all tourists to Florida were driving down. Aviation technology had improved enormously during the war years and Miami was a natural beneficiary, both because of its distance from the northern cities its tourists came from and because it was already established as an aviation center. By 1953, Miami International Airport had become the world's greatest airport of entry. The airlines figured out a way to lure even more business: 1947 saw the first package plan, developed between Delta and an aging grand hotel of the twenties, the MacFadden-Deauville. Although it was a failure the first year, the package system steadily improved, especially after the new night flights substantially lowered costs. And with the perfection of air-conditioning

A big day: Pan American Airways puts its new four-engine, double-decked Clipper America on display, 1949.

after the war (it was actually invented during the thirties), bigger, more cost-efficient hotels could be constructed, housing tourists in summer as well as winter.

It was the summer tourist, the one who could never have afforded Miami Beach in the winter, to whom the package plan was pitched. Middle-income Americans were taking advantage of the fat years after World War II, enjoying the privileges of their small discretionary income and the new practice of paid vacations. The shoe salesman or secretary may not have had much to spend on a trip, but they were a huge new market waiting to be cornered. "You live in lazy luxury for seven wonderful days," purred the copywriter for a pamphlet selling Delta's Millionaire Summer Vacation. "You forget everything but having fun, from breakfast in bed in the morning to dancing at night on a patio cooled by ocean breezes, for Delta's one low-cost ticket covers this glorious

vacation." The price for a couple coming from Cincinnati, for example, was $130 per person.

Miami Beach was being merchandised, and part of the package was the hotel the tourist was going to be staying in. That was the innocent observation of Morris Lapidus, a New York architect who came to Miami Beach in 1949 to work on his first hotel, after years of designing commercial buildings. He realized that the object of both types of building was the same: to sell the product. "The guests want to find a new experience," he wrote in his autobiography, *An Architecture of Joy.* "Forget the office, the house, the kids, the bills. Anything but that good old homey feeling that the old hotels used to sell with a comfortable bed, a nice rocker on the veranda, a good solid, nourishing meal. Not on your life! We were coming out of the war and the postwar period. People wanted fun, excitement . . . the visual excitement that made people want to

Miami was the gateway to the exotic weekend worlds of the Caribbean and Central and South America. In 1952, when this photo was taken, more international travelers passed through the Miami Airport than New York's Idlewild.

buy—in this case, to buy the tropic luxury of a wonderful vacation of fun in the sun."

Lapidus, whose name would become synonymous with Miami Beach glamour and glitz, had grown up in the Williamsburg area of Brooklyn, the son of Russian Jewish immigrants. He had trained as an architect but dreamed of becoming an actor, and his designs for storefronts and their interiors, and later hotels, were inspired by his taste for theatrical techniques. Among his hallmarks were the use of color, sweeping curves, and strategic lighting, as well as three decorative forms—"woggles," suspended free-form shapes; slender floor-to-ceiling "bean poles"; and "cheese holes" cut into a ceiling or wall. One of his commerical clients introduced him to Ben Novack, who hired Lapidus in 1949 to "add some flairs" to his new Miami Beach hotel, the Sans Souci.

Lapidus had done some work on Catskills hotels during the war, where he noticed that the city dwellers who came to the mountains to vacation weren't there to go hiking. What they liked best was socializing and getting dressed up in the evening for the night's entertainment, and for this they did not want a rustic setting. Likewise, the wave of tourists coming to Miami Beach after the war, many of whom were the same Catskills regulars, didn't come simply for the weather. They wanted to show off—their new success, their new clothes, their jewels (often rented), and their Cadillac convertibles. The Miami Beach tourist came to be entertained, and where once sports and tea dances, and, later, gambling casinos and nightclubs, had filled the bill, Lapidus had the idea to make the hotel itself part of the amusements.

Lapidus's work in Miami Beach was a marked departure from previous Beach styles—the grand-hotel tradition of the Roney Plaza or the sweet make-believe of the homey Deco hotels, or even the tastefully dramatic 1941 Shelbourne, a Bauhaus-inspired design whose broad, airy lobby opened to a view of the palm trees and beach. But Lapidus's theatrical bent, his "showiness," as some derogatorily put it, followed a Florida architectural tradition established by architects like Joseph Urban, a former Ziegfeld Follies set designer, who was responsible for the fabulous and florid Mar-a-Lago in Palm Beach, and his local competitor Addison Mizner, *fantasiste extraordinaire*.

For his 1949 interiors for the Sans Souci, Lapidus concentrated on creating an artificial environment that stimulated the guests' fantasies of a luxurious life of leisure. As he wrote in his autobiography, *An Architecture of Joy*:

Once again, I used my old bag of tricks—sweeping curves, a woggle-shaped carpet, the old cheese holes in the floating ceiling and the curved walls, bean poles on which hung bird cages with live birds. . . . There were native coral stone walls with splashing fountains and lush tropical foliage growing in the most unlikely places. There was a grand circular stairway. Terraces that went up and then went down for no special reason, just an exuberance of motion. Colors were splashed over the interiors as well as the exterior. . . . In the gardens and on the pool deck, colored lighting turned the areas into an exotic fairyland. All of this might be called artificial and flamboyant by the purists, but who cared? It was colorful and exciting—it was fun. And that was what I reasoned a resort hotel should be selling and sell it did.

Hotels were all the rage after the Sans Souci. Every new hotel vied to be This Year's Hotel, the current status-symbol address. There was plenty of competition for the title. In the ten years after the war, three dozen hotels were built on Collins Avenue between Lincoln Road and the Firestone Estate, on Forty-fourth Street. Up the oceanfront they climbed, squeezing themselves in between the few older hotels—the Algiers, Delmonico, DeLido, Monte Carlo, Casablanca, Sorrento, San Marino, Lombardy; the Sherry-Frontenac, Martinique, Versailles; the Coronet, Sovereign, Empress, Patrician, Embassy; the Sea Isle, Coral Reef, Atlantic Towers, Sea Gull, Shoremede, Triton; the Surrey and the Cadillac, among them. The name was clearly an important element in the hotel's appeal. David Levenson, who built the Algiers, said that Lapidus, who did the interiors, had helped them come up with a name that they could design the hotel around. "We wanted something on top of the alphabet and something with a theme and something with a little history behind it," said Levenson, a name recipe that most of the new hotels more or less followed.

In the mid-forties, you could still see the Atlantic between the hotels and the surviving oceanfront mansions as you drove up Collins. But this new building boom transformed Miami Beach. Once the hotels had 40-60-80 rooms, now they had 150-200-250 rooms. In order to compete with the glamorous new hotels, smaller prewar hotels started modernizing their lobbies and coffee shops, putting flocked wallpaper over a Deco mural here, hanging a kidney-shaped woggle there. They added stories, squeezed new wings into their side lots, and built sweeping drives in front of the entrance. By the fifties, the Collins Avenue of old—palmy, breezy, scattered with coconuts and scented by jasmine—had been transformed into a crazy concrete wall of hotels. Writer Edmund Wilson made a trip to Miami and described it in his book *Red, Black, Blond and Olive*.

I have never been here before and am astounded and appalled by this place. It is not that it is particularly different from other American seaside resorts . . . but that here both the cheap and the expensive aspects have been developed on a scale that I have never elsewhere seen equalled. You have acres of nougat-like shops, mountain-ranges of vanilla ice-cream hotels.

And he hadn't seen anything yet.

THE BATTLE FOR THE BEACH

Architect Morris Lapidus employed his "moth theory," using spots of illumination and brilliant colors to draw guests to the Sans Souci's public areas. The Harlequin Bar (opposite) and a lobby area (below).

If the public had their view of the ocean cut off, they were at least compensated by this ever-changing architectural display. What was happening behind the hotels was more disturbing—the buildings were expanding toward and sometimes beyond the shoreline, obstructing the public's legal access to the beach and hastening the natural erosion process.

In the twenties, the city established a line along the high-water mark on all oceanfront land at which point property

owners could build a bulkhead—a concrete or steel wall—to protect their land against the ocean. The beach land east of the bulkhead was public property. It also became common to construct low walls, called "groins," which extended into the ocean, perpendicular to the beach, for perhaps two hundred feet. The groins were supposed to protect a particular stretch of beach from being washed away by the waves and perhaps to build up the beach by trapping sand washed up onto it.

Ultimately these practices turned out to exacerbate erosion. Waves bouncing hard off the bulkhead carried away sand, and groins prevented sand from moving naturally down the shoreline. So while one man's beach might have been protected by a groin, his neighbor's was being deprived of replenishment, and eventually everyone had a neighbor with a groin. No one understood where the sand came from, and that they were defeating their purpose by building the barriers. The problem became more obvious as the decades passed; the beach diminished, at points disappeared.

The public was also in danger of losing access to the existing beach. The modest development ethic the city once had was compromised in the postwar building boom. The city council bent over backward to give hotel owners whatever they wanted to bring in more tourist dollars, and what hotel owners wanted was swimming pools, the postwar rage. To satisfy this swimming pool mania, hotel owners needed more space behind their property to build them.

Before his biggest triumphs, Lapidus sharpened his Miami Beach hotel style on several hotel interiors: the Sans Souci card room, the Algiers lobby, the Nautilus lobby.

One by one, hotel people requested and were granted permits by the city council to move their bulkhead seventy-five feet east of the existing limit. A setback ordinance from the thirties that required open space between the hotel and the bulkhead had also been weakened. Now hotel owners could improve the new area with swimming pools and cabanas built on a sand-filled, steel-walled box that sometimes extended so far out that it was standing in deep water even at low tide. At points, the public could not walk along the beach. Sometimes the only way a hotel guest could get to the sea was by climbing down steps built from the top of the deck.

In 1953, as a result of a suit that Miami Beach lawyer (later mayor) Melvin Richard filed against the city, a circuit court judge ordered a permanent injunction against the Miami Beach City Council forbidding it to ever again allow a developer to build across the public beach. Brazenly the city continued to issue variances to hotel and apartment builders to build into the sea. Waves lapped at the foundations of oceanfront buildings, storms regularly flooded hotel basements and the sublobby shopping arcades of the fifties, and the shoreline was buried under steel and concrete.

NIGHTCLUB ROW

Everything on Miami Beach became bigger and bolder after the war. Money had never been spent quietly in Miami Beach, but it became even more conspicuous in the late forties, and that was part of the entertainment. The guilty price-tag-watching of the war years had turned positively celebratory. Articles cheerfully noted that a Miami Beach vacationer could pay $1,500 for a necktie (no one ever bought these ties, but one store stocked them for years just for the publicity) or that $2 million was dropped at the racetracks on a good day. The social life of the big hotels centered around the swimming pool, although actual swimming was déclassé. The women arrived carefully made up and wearing the latest fashion swimsuit—"It may be some little thing of pure silk costing only $45, but it may also be a creation of gold-trimmed velvet or sequins and ermine at $145," wrote Life in 1947—as well as some cunning garment that transformed the suit into party- or streetwear. Money, flesh, and self-indulgence gave the Beach an atmosphere of "uninhibited paganism," said Life.

Nightlife was booming—the ten years after the war were probably the best for entertainment, according to locals. Dade Boulevard was nightclub row. There was Ciro's and the Paddock Club, which was run by Ralph "Bottles" Capone, Al's brother ("You didn't think of them as gangsters," said one Beachite. "I never knew of any mobster activities. No one offered me dope or anything!"); the Beachcomber; Mother Kelly's, where Helen Morgan fended off lounge lizards by claiming she was going home with Mother, Robert Kelly; and Kitty Davis's Airliner, shaped like the inside of a hangar (as explained in her life story on the place mat, she believed that in the future large stratoliners would have regular nightclub entertainment). When Kitty Davis's closed, Michel Rosenberg's Little Roumania ("The food was good, but the jokes Scandinavian") opened on the same spot, featuring entertainment by Jan Bart, "Jovial Songster"; Atta Boy Getzel, "Yiddish Story Teller"; Chet Clark, "Harmonicat"; and the Johnny Silvers Orchestra. The classy joints were the Copa, which supplied little hammers on the table for applauding, in the Catskills tradition, and the Palm Island Club, run by Lou Walters, Barbara Walters's father. Near the Roney were Bill Jordan's Bar of Music and the Five O'Clock Club, at one time owned by Martha Raye, where everyone met after work for 45-cent cocktails. At Murray Franklin's, the host greeted guests at the door by unzipping his fly, pulling out a huge stem-winder watch, and yelling, "Hey! You're late." The Dempsey-Vanderbilt Hotel had an outdoor club where Jack Dempsey would present the guests with small golden boxing gloves as favors.

The Algiers was actually flat up against Collins Avenue, but its promotional brochure was as imaginative as the hotel.

The Cohens in the penthouse suite of their Martinique Hotel, the Beach's first completely air-conditioned hotel. "In the early days," said a local, "you could sit in the lobbies and smell the freon."

The Hotel Ivanhoe pool. By the postwar years, bigger and ever more distinctive pools became the center of hotel life. Even pool counting was a preoccupation: according to one report, between 1945 and 1955 the number of pools in the city went from 134 to 466, an increase of 247.7 percent.

The Raleigh Hotel pool, considered the Beach's prettiest even when it was no longer its newest.

Kitty Davis's nightclub was decorated to look like the inside of a plane.

The famous Five O'Clock Club.

Club and restaurant matchbooks.

The big new hotels each had their "rooms" whose atmosphere and decor were largely inspired by Havana, the wild weekend destination that made Miami Beach's nightlife look like prom entertainment. Vying for the rhumba enthusiast's attention: the Burgundy Room at the Sands Hotel ("The rhumba one spot!") or the Raleigh Patio, featuring Manolo and Ethel, Exponents of the Dance . . . Monday-night rhumba contests at the Ritz Plaza and at the Atlantis Hotel with Monchito and His Suavicito 8-Piece Orchestra, as well as "cocktail dansants" . . . the Sapphire Room at the Belmar Hotel with Juanito Sanabria's orchestra . . . the Starlight Patio at the Caribbean Hotel with Tony Negrett and "his authentic Cubans." Desi Arnaz, who had lived with his aunt while going to grade school on the Beach, came back in the forties as a bandleader. Playing the lounge of the fancy Park Avenue Restaurant, he'd start a conga line that would snake through the restaurant.

The Beach also had a thriving gay scene, and bars with drag shows, like the Echo Club, the Circus Club, and the Jewel Box, were illicit tourist attractions. Some of the gay bars were on Alton Road, some below Fifth Street and around the Twenty-third Street beach, a longtime gay area. For the uninitiated reader, 1942's *The Saint in Miami* described the exoticisms of Miami nightlife. The Saint and his date take a long drive out to a nightclub called the Palmleaf Fan, "a rambling Spanish-type bungalow" hidden away somewhere in an undeveloped area of Miami. A nightclub with gambling in a back room, it might have been inspired by Greenacres, a low-down type of gambling casino that attracted the high rollers.

It dawned on him in passing that some of the groups of highly made-up girls who sat at inferior tables with an air of hoping to be invited to better ones were a trifle sinewy in the arms and neck, while on the other hand some of the delicate-featured young men who sat apart from them were too well-developed in the chest for the breadth of their shoulders. Those eccentricities were standard in the honky-tonks of Miami.

THE BUSINESS OF GAMBLING

Gambling was the main social activity. Like everything else, the gambling that had been done in elite casinos in the thirties expanded to embrace the masses. Besides the pari-mutuel betting at Hialeah, at the other horse and dog tracks, and at the jai-alai fronton, there were still plenty of gambling casinos—the Royal Palm Club in Miami, the Brook Club and the Colonial Inn in Surfside, the Island Club in Sunny Isles, to name a few—with a fancy floor show in the front room and roulette wheels spinning in the back room.

Local lawmakers and -keepers continued a "liberal policy"

The combination of open gambling and nightclub engagements drew celebrities to the Beach in the forties and early fifties. Joan Crawford.

Jimmy Durante, Mayor Marcie Liberman, and nightclub owner Murray Franklin.

The Ritz Brothers (second, third, and fifth from left).

Ann Sheridan, rumored to have secretly eloped with head Miami Beach publicist Steve Hannagan.

Carmen Miranda.

Elizabeth Taylor.

Jerry Lewis with the Vagabonds.

toward gambling. That is, Miami Beach was wide open, so much so that *Life* could matter-of-factly write that the Miami Beach police department made raids only at the end of the season, and competition between rival casino operators was front-page news in the local newspapers. The idea of law enforcement could even be turned to a gambler's advantage. According to a 1952 article in the journal *Tequesta*, one man, "by judicious use of folded money," employed hawkers for a little-known newspaper named *Miami Life* to stand in front of crowded Beach hotels and yell, "'Gambling running wide open at such-and-such club,' using the name of his establishment. There was nothing about that in the papers they carried, but the stunt filled his gambling rooms."

Every hotel had a resident bookie, either at the lobby cigar stand or in a special cabana by the pool. "Horse parlors were plush, spacious, air-conditioned and accessible to all major bus and jitney lines," a small-time gambler named Sid Morris rem-

inisced in an article in *The Thoroughbred Record*. "A patron was greeted at the door or cabana flap with an invitation to indulge in a hot corned beef sandwich with pickle or fresh fruits and cakes and the beverage of his choice." The hotel bookmaking concession was an important part of the financial life of the hotels. Typically, somebody who wanted to build an ocean-front hotel got four or five men together to pool their resources. But since there was never enough money, each owner would sell pieces of his or her interest to subowners, and if there still wasn't enough, and there usually wasn't, they'd rent out a bookmaking concession in the lobby and/or a cabana for a down payment plus a good monthly rent. The retainer for a cigar-stand concession could run as high as $20,000, money that had to be put up by a big-time gambler, the "bankroll."

Almost every hotel had this money coming in to help it operate. But it wasn't always a voluntary arrangement. When

ROBERTO
MEXICANA BAR
10th & Collins Ave,
Miami Beach, Fla

Several popular night spots on the Beach and Miami's Biscayne Boulevard featured drag-queen entertainment and clients. A postcard from the Roberto Mexicana Bar on Collins and Tenth Street.

125

One of many "rooms" in the city, where bookies took bets and tracked races all over the country.

John Weiner's family got into the hotel business in Miami—they also owned White Roe Lake resort in the Catskills—the mob muscled in. Weiner's father hadn't permitted gambling in his Catskills hotel, not even a pinball machine, "because he knew that once you allow gambling, you lose control of the property," Weiner recalled. "But it was different in Miami Beach. Everybody gambled.

"This is how it worked," said Weiner. "A guy walked in and said, Okay, Weiner, we're giving you $5,000 for the book—my cousin, the first year, said he didn't want anything to do with a library—and the syndicate installed a bookmaker in your hotel, usually in a cabana.

"One year the season was bad, and the bookie told my cousin that he wanted $2,000 back; my cousin said a deal was a deal, and he got roughed up a little. One of the syndicate bosses called up and apologized, said they were a couple of new guys from Chicago, but still, they got their $2,000."

The efficiency of the system was due to the enterprising efforts of a local outfit called the S & G syndicate. No one knows what the initials stand for; some said "stop and go," for the manner in which their operations were interrupted by the law.

The S & G was a group of four local bookies who got together in 1944 to make a business out of financing other bookmakers. By 1948, the syndicate later reported in Senate hearings, it was grossing over $26 million in bets through its concessions at two hundred hotels—more than was being brought in by legal pari-mutuel betting—and netting somewhere between $2 and $8 million. Their existence was tolerated by the city. They even had an office on Lincoln Road with "S & G" printed on the frosted-glass door. Unlike independent bookies, bookies who belonged to the S & G were seldom raided, and if they did get busted, they only got fines and rarely went to jail. The system worked so smoothly that the city could figure into its annual budget a couple of hundred thousand dollars in fines and forfeitures.

By 1949, betting had risen to $40 million, and the syndicate had bookies in practically every hotel. "Along Collins Avenue so many radios blared race results so loudly that pedestrians could walk a mile without missing a single Win, Place or Show," wrote Polly Redford. The atmosphere was charged with odds-laying fever. The South Beach bookies hung out at Hoffman's Cafeteria in the evening, taking bets on that night's baseball game in Flamingo Park. The Miami Beach Flamingos, a bush-league baseball team, played Cuban teams stocked with players with names like Cabby Caballero, Chico Maria, and Pepper Martin. While waiting for the latest newspaper results, the countermen might quote the stuffed kishka at 9 to 11.

Anybody from a soda jerk to a family man could become a bookie and mix almost imperceptibly with the tourists; the only distinguishing trademark of a bookie was that they kept their collars buttoned rather than open. It was a job. Likewise, the members of the S & G were regarded as respectable citizens who brought money into the community and contributed to local charities. Business was rolling right along until out-of-town gangsters tried to muscle in on the S & G's territory. The gangsters who had been part of the scene since Capone's arrival in the late twenties were now firmly entrenched. Frank Erickson ran his extensive Florida bookmaking operations from the Wofford Hotel. Other out-of-town mobsters—among them Joe Adonis and Meyer and Jake Lansky—were operating big casinos in Broward and Dade counties. Gangsters had begun to buy up hotels, not just "invest" in them, particularly around the Twenty-third Street area. The Wofford catered to gangsters from around the country; the Sands was run by a Cleveland mobster, Alfred "Big Al" Polizzi, and two bookies from Philadelphia, and was frequented by Philadelphia gangsters; and the Grand was the favorite hangout for the Detroit Purple Gang. In fact, the area between the Grand and the Wofford became known around the country as a meeting place for nationally known racketeers and gangsters. "Little Cicero," it was sometimes called, after its sister neighborhood near Chicago, possessed a "certain homicidal glamour," as one Beachite reminisced.

Gambler Frank Costello, who walked out of the Senate crime hearings and retreated to Miami Beach, is seen here with Walter Winchell.

Senator Estes Kefauver made Miami's Dade County a focus of his investigation into inter-state organized crime.

In 1949, the Chicago-Capone syndicate forced the S & G to sell one of its members a one-sixth interest in the multimillion-dollar operation for a mere $20,000. The possibility of further infiltration by the mob sparked alarm in some local officials. "One of these days," warned Daniel Sullivan, of the Greater Miami Crime Commission, in a speech to members of the Committee of 100, "we might wake up to find that Dade County is completely in the power of these people." "Honest millionaires squirmed" as Sullivan showed slides of homes on the best streets in the city owned by such former associates of Al Capone's as Nick Delmore, Sam di Carlo, Joe Massei, John and Fred Angersola (operating under the name King), Charles Fischetti, and Sam Taran. But disturbing as it might have been to have a racketeer neighbor, everyone ignored the deeper significance of the gambling, even the honest millionaires who enjoyed high-stakes bingo games at the Bath and Surf clubs. "You don't shoot Santa Claus," an upstanding citizen explained. One sheriff who chose not to enforce the law later protested that he had been elected on the "liberal ticket," and he was only giving the people what they wanted.

By the end of the 1940s, the depth of the criminal infiltration was coming to light. As Miami-area gambling became a national issue, state officials put pressure on local authorities to clean up. Then, in 1950, Senator Estes Kefauver came to Miami to begin hearings there as part of his nationwide investigation into interstate organized crime. The Kefauver Committee exposed the corrupt ties between the gambling interests and law-enforcement figures and public officials. Members of the Dade County sheriff's office and the Miami Beach police force routinely received bribes for protecting gambling in Miami and the Beach. "Ex-Deputy Patton testified that he received an extra-large pay-off for special protection on one occasion when a wealthy oil man was steered to the Golden Shores Club, where he lost $800,000 on two nights," Kefauver reported in *What I Found Out About the Miami Mob*.

After Kefauver brought the Beach's gambling situation to national attention, city officials were forced to crack down. A bookie in the midst of a raid at the Viking Hotel.

Real postwar bathing suits, with their skirted or girdlelike bottoms, weren't as attractive as these homemade publicity-shoot creations.

A souvenir illustrated "letter" from a popular forties nightclub, El Chico.

Dear . . .

This town is terrific.

It has everything anybody could even start to wish for. Climate, recreational facilities, beaches, night clubs—Hey! talking about night clubs; listen to the swell thing that happened to us the other day. We leave the beach about 4:30 and decide to go for a stroll. We amble west on 22nd Street, past palm trees and a pretty park when suddenly a building, with the sign "EL CHICO" on it, pops up. Night club, we guess, and then everybody starts to get thirsty. We're in slacks, though, and there's only about two bucks in the crowd so we poke our heads in, kind of dubious. "I'm George," says a young fellow, "and this is my partner, Paul. C'mon in." And we do.

Well, it's as pretty a spot as we've ever seen. There's Spanish murals, nice lighting effects, smart dance floor and stage, and everybody's friendly and informal.

Naturally, we just have to have a second drink— you know how it is—but as we never take much money to the beach we're a little worried. "How much are the drinks?" we ask the bartender. "35 cents," he says. We feel relieved. "But," he adds, this is 'Penny Cocktail Hour,' every day between five and six—so you get TWO drinks for 36 cents!" Can y' imagine?

There's a rhumba band playing and before we know it it's 6:30. "Where's a good place to eat?" we ask the young fellow who had introduced himself as George. "Right here," he smiles. "If the food's as good as the drinks," we say, "we'll be back in an hour."

"Try us," pipes up Paul. And we do.

We come back around 8:30 and there's a million things on the menu to choose from. Everybody has something different and we're all pleased as punch over the food. Music for dancing is great, too, and there's two bands, American and Cuban.

Well, I don't think we've ever had more fun. Everything clicked just perfectly and we've already been in El Chico a half dozen times this week. Tuesday we saw their Country Store night and it was a panic. When I tell you that some of us won a brassiere, a bunch of spinach, a baby carriage, and roller skates, and somebody else won a live calf, you can guess what sort of a time we had.

The perfect night club. Truly that's the only way we can describe it.

If you come down here, it's got to be your first stop. Positively!

The S & G went out of operation as a result of the hearings. Many of the casinos were shut down, and the crackdown even affected the bingo games at the Bath and Surf clubs. Although high-stakes card games and small-scale bookmaking still went on quietly in hotels and horse rooms, open gambling on Miami Beach was over. Some thought its demise would hurt business on the Beach, but in fact the good times were just beginning. Although the blue bloods and now the high rollers were moving on ("Gamblers were the best spenders and the hugest tippers we ever had," a Wolfie's waitress lamented, "even better than the black marketeers"), they were being replaced with millions of middle-class Americans.

Vacationland, USA:
1954–1969

Fabulous, fabulous. I've been around the United States and I've never seen anything so fabulous. So clean and beautiful with the palms and everything, just fabulous.

— Woman interviewed by WTVJ
on the new Lincoln Road Mall, 1957

A promotional stunt at the Fontainebleau Hotel.

Drive down Collins Avenue today, with its peeling hotel fronts, defunct neon signs, jumbled porches, makeshift parking lots, and numerous seedy souvenir stores, and it's hard to imagine it as the glamorous main drag of the city in the 1940s, 1950s, and 1960s. But a film clip from the early fifties—a camera was held in the backseat of a shiny white convertible as it drove the length of the avenue from South Beach to the big curve at Forty-fourth Street—showed a sleek, brilliant street. Several hotels made dramatic statements, including the Algiers, with a glass-walled dining room that jutted out over the sidewalk, and the Sans Souci, with its deep curved driveway framing a two-tiered fountain. Collins Avenue looked broader than it does now because there were fewer cars parked along the sides. In contrast to today's cement hardness, patches of greenery graced the fronts of the hotels and big palms lined the street. Many bright, striped awnings shaded hotel entrances and shop doorways. All the buildings were freshly painted, all the cars were shiny and new, and people walked along the sidewalks in crisp dresses and summer suits; "You wouldn't dream of walking into a hotel without hat and gloves," noted a former tourist.

At the time the clip was filmed, the tourist strip ended at the bend in Collins Avenue. A year or two later, in 1954, the car would have turned and all of that scenery would have been overshadowed by the sight of the shocking new Fontainebleau Hotel.

The Fontainebleau went up on the grounds of the Firestone Estate, one of the oldest and most famous properties on the island and a symbol of the best Carl Fisher had hoped for Miami Beach—that it become the winter residence of wealthy American industrialists, à la Palm Beach. But Fisher had seen the Beach veering from that course even before his death in 1939, accommodating thousands of tourists who were neither rich nor even, in his eyes, altogether American.

Most of Carl Fisher's midwestern millionaires were gone now. As the real-estate market boomed after the war, they had quietly sold their oceanfront properties to investors who anticipated a zoning change that would increase their value more than fivefold. The new owners of the Firestone property had bulldozed the high walls and thick foliage that had long hidden the grounds from public view, and anybody who wanted to could now drive over and peek inside the big granite mansion, which had been made headquarters for the construction crew. Rising up behind it was the skeleton of a mammoth fourteen-story building in the form of a quarter-circle, destined to be, as its owner once proclaimed it, "the world's most pretentious hotel."

The Firestone Estate, whose sunken gardens were once a standard image on hand-tinted linen postcards, was being replaced with a hotel worthy of a Technicolor movie. Coming down was the symbol of what was considered the Beach's high-class, blueblood heritage. Going up in its stead: "a very classy place." The Fontainebleau was designed to represent old-world luxury to its recently rich clientele, people who'd

Fabulous Miami Beach

made good through a new era of American prosperity, just as Carl Fisher and his friends had at the turn of the century. These new visitors to Miami Beach were not as wealthy, of course, but there were many more of them, and they wanted their own version of the grand hotels and the polo ponies. In a way, not much had changed.

Author Thomas Hine coined the word "populuxe"—synthetic, popular, luxurious, and classy—to describe the peculiar American aesthetic that characterized the years between 1954 and 1964. "People wanted to be known for their good taste," he wrote in *Populuxe,* "but they also wanted to have great showy things that demonstrated that they had

The Fontainebleau under construction. Architect Morris Lapidus salvaged part of the formal gardens of the Firestone Estate to enhance the hotel's "modern French provincial" ambience.

arrived. Populuxe is vulgar by definition. It is the result of an unprecedented ability to acquire, reaching well down into the working class. . . . These people did not acquire the good simple objects many tastemakers advocated. They had had it with simple, and now they wanted more."

Architect Morris Lapidus and Ben Novack, the owner of the Fontainebleau, were the men to give it to them—Lapidus because he knew how to package the product, a useful talent in the new consumer economy, and Novack because he, like his clientele, had no cultural pretensions. Lapidus designed a sleek, contemporary structure, to which Novack attached the name "Fontainebleau"—he and his wife had driven by the

The International Style as interpreted by Morris Lapidus.

Château Fontainebleau and he thought the name was catchy. To go with it, he wanted the interiors to be that "real luxury modern French provincial."

Lapidus made the most out of the French provincial dictate. He reasoned that the biggest influence on the tastes of the typical Miami Beach tourist was the movies, especially the Depression-era fantasies the tourists had grown up on. So Lapidus did what he liked doing best: he designed a stage set, and he incorporated the kind of techniques used by Busby Berkeley—vast spaces, dramatic entrances, a swirling grand staircase—with the luxurious materials and king-sized furniture that would best approximate real luxury modern French provincial.

The Fontainebleau gave its patrons everything they had dreamed of, and then some. Press members, flown down by private plane for a five-day junket when the hotel opened, were barraged with statistics: 49,000 square yards of carpeting, 2,000 mirrors, 22 carloads of furniture and antiques, 200 phones, 847 employees—1.4 per guest. The hotel was almost wall-to-wall marble, including white marble floors with a black bow-tie pattern, pink marble columns, and dozens of pieces of marble statuary scattered about the public spaces—"I am probably responsible for the rejuvenation of marble in this country," Novack later claimed. Walking up and down New York's Third Avenue antique district with a $100,000 budget, Lapidus had picked out the gold-trimmed antique piano, the

Louis XV armoires, the gilt-framed mirrors, and the crystal chandeliers that now adorned the hotel interiors—"When the dealers saw Morris," it was said, "they thought they saw God." Waiters' jackets and bed pillows were sprinkled with the fleur-de-lis, and the bedroom wallpaper featured scenes of Paris. The closets, including a cedar closet for furs, were twice the size of a normal hotel closet; no one needed that much space, but it gave guests a feeling that they were the kind of people who *could* fill it.

Behind the hotel, Lapidus put in a four-acre French parterre, a children's swimming pool shaped like a pussycat, and another pool 60 feet wide by 120 feet long; the 1958 Frank Sinatra movie *Hole in the Head* filmed a waterskiing sequence in it. The pool had windows at either end so people in the lower lobby or at the bar in the Poodle Lounge could watch swimmers kick their legs, adjust their suits, or, what Truman Capote got a kick out of, see them urinate underwater. An S-shaped cabana colony lined the beach; with two and three rooms apiece, the cabanas were virtual suites, and during the good times, guests occasionally were put up in them.

The Fontainebleau was expensive—in 1954, the cheapest room was $83 a day and a penthouse suite cost $135—and the cost of maintaining the Fontainebleau lifestyle became legendary. One Texas millionaire was said to have spent $100,000 for rooms and a cabana for a season. Gin rummy players by the pool could lose four or five hundred dollars in an ordinary day,

The "Staircase to Nowhere"—it connected the lobby to a small mezzanine—became a trademark of the Lapidus hotel.

OPPOSITE: "Spongecake is spongecake," Lapidus once said. "The frosting sells the cake." The lobby of the Fontainebleau.

A reception in the Fontainebleau's French parterre gardens. Formality was the keynote of a Miami Beach vacation in the fifties and sixties.

and the Mad Russian—he ate caviar with a soup spoon—once lost $20,000.

The hotel lobby served as a kind of open-air display case for one's personal effects. Men were required to wear a jacket and tie to sit there in the evening, and the proper "lobby dress" could run to $600. Fur stoles were de rigueur, even in the afternoon, even if it was just a little breath-of-spring mink (its pale beige color was achieved by feeding a young mink chemicals) to wear while you were slumming on Collins Avenue. The slogan "Bring your trunks empty," a promotion for Lincoln Road shopping, took on new meaning as status-conscious tourists began hauling around empty pieces of luggage in order to look sufficiently loaded. If you didn't have the proper acces-

sories when you got to the hotel, you could buy them in the posh shopping arcade beneath the lobby level, where the stores were open past midnight. "You'd be surprised how many women feel like buying a four-hundred-and-fifty-dollar mink-trimmed sweater in the middle of the night," a store manager said at the time.

Diamonds were the ultimate status symbol. "I once got a call from a tourist who asked me how many diamonds it was permissible to wear to lunch," said a former fashion coordinator for Burdine's department store. "So I told her what she wanted to hear: If you've got 'em, flaunt 'em." Ruth Katz, a tourist from Long Island, remembered seeing diamonds for the first time at the Fontainebleau. "Getta loada that ice," her girlfriend whispered during an Edith Piaf performance, nodding toward a woman seated near them. "Once you've seen real diamonds," Ruth confided, "you're never fooled by rhinestones again."

Of course, if you really ran with the fast crowd, you didn't stay at the Fontainebleau, you rented your own place. An article in the Miami *Herald* gleefully tallied up how much you'd have to spend to be part of the 1954 "glitter set": "You Might Get By for $35,000." That would cover the cost of staying in Miami Beach for the entire four-month season, figuring in a two-bedroom apartment, servants, two Cadillacs, private club fees, some cocktail parties, nightclub outings, a mink, an ermine, cocktail dresses, beaded cashmere sweaters, a few "cabana sets" (a bathing suit or play togs with a matching cover-up) and tuxedos, a box at Hialeah, and a decent-sized cruiser.

The success of the Fontainebleau brought Lapidus a commission in 1955 to build a hotel right next door. "Hey," said his new client, Morris Lansburgh, when Lapidus attempted to foist a contemporary style upon him, "My guests aren't kids just out of school! You must have something besides French. How about Italian Renaissance?"

The Eden Roc, though smaller, was deemed by many to be even classier than the Fontainebleau. Running the full height of the building were two vertical mosaic tile panels, gradated from deep to pale turquoise. Brass gaslights were planted by the entrance, and a whimsical ship's stack, which hid the service unit, sailed merrily away on the roof. Oval-shaped rosewood columns, holding up neoclassical woggles, defined the lobby seating area, and a curved, two-story wall of windows draped with tucked fabric framed the rear of the room. The furniture was lavender and blue, with black-and-white terrazzo floors. Fragments of Ionic columns appeared as stands for lamps and bronze sculptures, as door handles to the nightclub, and as the four points of the clock over the check-in desk. "If ever I designed an elegant movie set as a lobby for a grand hotel, this was it," said Lapidus.

But the ultimate Lapidus hotel was the Americana, which opened the following year in Bal Harbour, just north of Miami Beach. Although Lapidus had been creating artificial environments in Miami Beach since the Sans Souci, this was his first artificial tropical environment. A huge funnel-shaped terrarium open to the sky dominated the lobby; inside was a sculpted mountain with a waterfall, tropical foliage, and a few small alligators. The whole miniature jungle was rigged to be showered with a hundred gallons of water every two hours, and to glow with artificial moonlight at night. This time the hotel's theme was the Americas, carried out in such features as twenty-foot-high mosaic murals of the great explorers and a huge "Mayan" screen made of bits of Venetian glass, wood, and brass that encircled the lobby. The Dominion Coffee Shop was decorated with totem poles, and the waitresses' outfits were patterned after Jeanette MacDonald's *Rose Marie* costumes. Back in the Southern Hemisphere, two thousand tons of coral rock had been hauled in and assembled around the patio and pool area.

The Americana made Lapidus an even more conspicuous target than his earlier hotels. One critic, referring to the jarring, sawtoothed arrangement of balconies, said that every room had a view of the ocean, you just needed a periscope to see it. Ada Louise Huxtable, the *New York Times* architecture critic, remarked that the Lapidus-designed bellboy uniforms in black, yellow, and purple made her feel like she'd been hit by an exploding eggplant. Those were the usual barbs. Then there were the brutal frontal attacks. When the American Institute of Architects held its 1963 convention at the hotel, with Lapidus in attendance, one architect called the Americana "incompetent, uncomfortable and a monument to vulgarity."

Despite the scorn of the critics, the tourists loved the Lapidus hotels, and every developer in town jumped on the theme bandwagon. Most found that a catchy name and a few decorative touches went a long way toward capturing a tourist's attention and stimulating his or her escapist fantasies. The Seville Hotel—Café Olé, Matador Room, Cha-Cha Bar—had gold-tiled columns in the lobby and bedrooms with

They must be on their way to the Eden Roc's Mona Lisa Room.

OPPOSITE:

Ben Novack, owner of the Fontainebleau, never forgave Lapidus or former partner Harry Mufson for opening the Eden Roc next door. It was a vision of the Italian Renaissance in purple, blue, and gold and was considered to be an even more elegant hotel.

fuschia-pink walls patterned with matadors. Skiers schussed down the walls of the Swiss Lounge at the Lucerne Hotel (Alpine dining room, William Tell coffee shop, Club Chalet nightclub).

On Collins Avenue, in Sunny Isles, a hundred blocks north of the Fontainebleau, dozens of motels had sprung up that catered to the tourists, usually young families, who could not afford glamorous Miami Beach. The motels were kitsch car-

toons that advertised themselves not just with a sign but with a symbol, perfect for the young consumer who could not read. The Sahara had two stuffed camels and a stuffed Arab at the entrance. Water pouring off the roof spun a huge wagon wheel at the Old Sun Ranch. The Chateau had a steep-pitched roof and white half-timbers set into pink stucco (château, chalet, what's the difference?). Most alluring of them all was the Cast-aways, a South Pacific motor village set on its own little

OPPOSITE: *Lapidus wanted to put monkeys in the Americana's tropical terrarium. The Tisches, who owned the hotel, wouldn't let him.*

LEFT: *Lapidus described the far wall here in the Americana as something "the Aztecs would have done if they had thought of it."*

BELOW: *The floor of the Americana's Carioca Lounge was inspired by the sidewalk of the Copacabana in Rio.*

The much-photographed carport at the Casablanca Hotel, forerunner to the exteriors of dozens of family-oriented motels in nearby Sunny Isles.

dredged island, featuring a moon gate, teahouse, Japanese gardens, subterranean Shipwreck Bar, and a compound of motel barracks with Polynesian-style roofs.

If the roadside gimmickry didn't snare you, the advertising would. The Chateau published a tantalizing pamphlet in the sixties that zeroed in on its finer selling points: the pink doors; the walkway in the grass made of odd-sized cement circles, pink, pale yellow, and white; the lily pond with a tiny arched bridge that graced the back of the hotel. The rooms had pink-and-gray-striped carpet, pink vinyl furniture, beds with pink coverlets, a table surrounded by pink ice-cream-parlor chairs, and a pot of plastic ivy trailing off the top of the TV. "**You'll revel** in the French Provincial luxury of your CHATEAU guest room," read the captions splashed across the pictures. "**Imagine** yourself in this luxurious CHATEAU Kitchenette Apartment!" And then, "**For your dining pleasure** . . . it's the Chatelaine Room!" with pink-clothed tables, sunburst-patterned carpet, and a table set with a display of wines surrounding a flower centerpiece set on top of a cake stand. Gooey, deli-quality pies and cakes, half-eaten, represented "your choice of superb foods, cooked to a king's taste by the CHATEAU's renowned chefs!"

"Le Château! C'est Magnifique!"

The Sahara Motel's copywriter had more flair, although, of course, more theme to work with:

IF A REAL LIVE GENIE could make your every wish for a perfect vacation come true . . . she'd transport you to the Sahara, Miami Beach's number one resort. An ideal location only an abracadabra away from shopping, theatres, race tracks, jai-alai.

Resort sorcery . . . pleasure and practicality combined. Right on premises, there's free parking, beauty and sundry shops, self-service laundry, free sightseeing and fishing. . . .

Disappear from the dull . . . reappear at the real resort, **The Sahara**.

Whether it was intentional or not, an article in *Architectural Forum* put a cruel twist on Lapidus's assessment of hotelkeeping as show business; hotels as stage sets. Illustrated with four pages of photographs of the local flora and fauna—fake classical sculptures, a concrete sphinx with breasts, the higgledy-piggledy streetscape of Collins Avenue—the article was called "Miami Beach: Dream Dump, U.S.A."

"This was the final dumping ground . . . the dream dump," Nathanael West wrote to describe the lot in back of a big Hollywood studio, where old, bedraggled movie sets were piled up for storage. He might have been speaking of Miami Beach in 1959, an 8-square-mile repository for today's dreams and yesterday's nightmares, a vast sales counter bristling with slightly worn mechanisms of escape. . . . This is the final dumping ground—for throw-away architecture.

It was bad enough that "throw-away architecture" was the height of fashion in Miami Beach—it was being exported to New York City. When Lapidus's S-shaped Summit Hotel, now Loew's New York, opened in midtown Manhattan, critics heaped abuse on it. "Let's not have any more snake dances on Lexington Avenue," one wrote. "A nice hotel," said another, "but too far from the beach." Huxtable, with a nod to Lapidus's sense of humor and his understanding of the "pop mentality," summed up his work as "uninspired superschlock." Lapidus was stamped "Miami Beach architect" and shelved.

Even while the architectural establishment was getting its licks in, Lapidus's work was receiving a more gentle, if slightly patronizing, assessment by a new generation of architects and critics interested in what was being called "vernacular" architecture. They tended to agree with Lapidus's own assessment of his work: that the success of his buildings should be judged by their popularity with the public. Their "supergraphic" billboard exteriors, as he has called them, and theatrical, set-decorative interiors were appropriate forms for buildings

The Mammoth
Marzipan–style
of Motel Mile:
the Bonaire and
the Blue Mist.

designed to house people on two-week vacations. They were also, not incidentally, well-designed service institutions.

With the passage of time and extensive remodeling, the Lapidus hotels have almost assimilated. For most of its guests these days, the Fontainebleau is a famous name attached to a class A, Hilton chain hotel, with more marble, less brass-and-glass. Compared to the startling new high rises across the bay or to the grandiose Portman hotels, the Lapidus hotels no longer appear particularly extravagant. They are simply what their architect designed them to be: places for having fun.

"WHY NOT?"

Miami Beach tourists, meanwhile, suffered no conflicts about their extravagant island paradise. They didn't think it was too much—they couldn't get enough of it. "Miami Beach was built for big-city people," one publicist was quoted as saying. "It's the big city's idea of a tropical setting. Furthermore, it's primarily a Jewish resort. The reason Jews like Miami Beach is because it's a resort that says, 'Indulge yourself, live a little.' Drive out to the Bonfire restaurant and have a piece of their chocolate cake. It's about a foot high. Sure, nobody needs this, but that's Miami Beach. Wolfie's delicatessen has pastrami sandwiches three inches thick—it's kind of a symbol. So if the hotels seem overplush—why not?"

Two and a half million tourists were coming to the Miami area every year during the fifties, and most of them were staying on the Beach. The hotel count had grown from 291 in 1942 to 382 in 1955; the city's public relations director claimed that more hotels had been built in Miami Beach since the war than in the rest of the world combined. Each year at least one bigger, presumably better, and always more expensive hotel made its debut. The Hotels of the Year 1957, the Carillon and the Deauville, were booked solid before they even opened.

Some warned that the Beach was overdeveloped, to which the cry went up, "Miami Beach isn't overbuilt; it's *under-promoted!*"

Publicity had been the key to Miami Beach's success since Carl Fisher's time. Fisher brought down a young man named Steve Hannagan who'd worked for him at the Indianapolis Speedway to head the new resort's publicity department. Under Hannagan, who went on to become a successful Hollywood agent, the Miami Beach publicity machine grew into a smooth-running industry. Hannagan took pains to make sure that Miami Beach was recognized in national news reports as a separate entity from Miami—or, rather, that all the good news about the area got a Miami Beach dateline and all the bad news got Miami's. One of his first press releases—"Flash—Julius Fleischmann just dropped dead on polo field here don't forget Miami Beach dateline"—hung in the UP office for years as an example of classic press agentry. And he gave Fisher's sun-sand-sex formula a slicker, wittier gloss. Hannagan made Miami Beach synonymous with wholesome bathing beauties by mailing dozens of photographs out to northern newspapers, which became a wintertime staple. When real tourists didn't fill the need for models, local high school girls were excused from classes as if it were their civic duty. The five newsreel companies sent cameramen down to the Beach each winter, too, where city publicists arranged for them to film stock activities like speedboat races, lifeguard rescues, and swimming performances before they got down to the main event: filming beautiful legs. Hannagan also got Walter Winchell, then the most popular columnist in the country, to come down. Winchell's columns did much to make Miami Beach and the Roney Plaza famous.

Celebrities were always corralled for some photos and quotes—Hollywood seems to have been especially well represented in the forties—but equally important was the local-yokel shot. Publicity-office photographers regularly met incoming flights and took pictures of Mr. and Mrs. So-and-So arriving in Miami, which they sent back to the couple's hometown newspaper. The paper loved getting it, the people loved

Miami Beach News Bureau photographer Chris Hansen made a career out of taking cheesecake photos for little newspapers across the country, spreading the message that Miami Beach was "a fun place to be." The photographer and models staging a gag at the Algiers Hotel.

getting their picture in the paper, and when they went home they bragged to everybody about the great time they had. Word of mouth was a powerful selling tool.

Stunts, such as Rosie the elephant caddying for Warren Harding, were another way of getting attention. In the fifties, after some gemlike decorations were made for the walls of the Aladdin nightclub in the Algiers Hotel, management announced that some big "jewels" were going to be displayed in the hotel and had them delivered in an armored truck. The Lord Tarleton's owner, Al Jacobs, got a phone call from the Ritz Brothers during high season in the early fifties, wanting to come down, and Jacobs said there wasn't any room. "You gotta make room," the comedians said, and when they arrived Jacobs showed them to some tents he'd put up on the beach behind the hotel. Pictures of the Ritz Brothers sticking out of a tent made all the papers.

Television added a new element to the public-relations mix. To understand the most important reason why the crowds were getting bigger, said the Miami *News*, "turn on your TV set. From Dave Garroway's show in the morning to Steve Allen's *Tonight*, 170 million people are being exposed to the picture of this balmy winter on Miami Beach." So popular was a broadcast from Miami Beach that Lucy and Ricky and Fred and Ethel took a vacation at a stage-set Eden Roc in a 1956 episode (lots of marlins being hidden in bathroom tubs).

Arthur Godfrey had taken up Walter Winchell's banner. Since 1953, Godfrey had been packing his ukelele and coming down for two weeks to a month, broadcasting TV and radio shows from the Kenilworth Hotel in Bal Harbour. His popularity was at a peak, and he plugged the city relentlessly as Vacationland, U.S.A. To express its appreciation, the city named Forty-first Street after him in the late fifties, inaugurating a new Miami Beach tradition of honoring its promoters with street dedications. Ed Sullivan Boulevard now stands as a

Arthur Godfrey, here with regular guests the McGuire Sisters, pioneered the remote TV broadcast from a Miami Beach hotel in 1950. His broadcasts were priceless publicity for the Beach.

The Life and Times of Miami Beach

LEFT: *Jackie Gleason and his variety-show entourage of 268 people arrived in Miami Beach in a private train, the Great Gleason Express. Gleason was king of the Beach while his variety show was on the air, from 1964 to 1969.*

OPPOSITE, TOP: *Dave Garroway, host of the* Today *show, broadcasting from the Americana.*

OPPOSITE, BOTTOM: *The Beatles ran up a $3,000 bill at the Deauville in swimsuits, cabana outfits, and other essential tourist paraphernalia during their four-day stay in 1964.*

reminder of his special broadcasts from the Beach, including his "really really big shew" there, a performance by the Beatles on their first American tour, held at the Deauville in 1964. The hotel thereafter charged special rates for the group's suite, 1111. Beatles gossip spread like wildfire through the small city. Their first night in town they escaped to the Peppermint Lounge on the Seventy-ninth Street Causeway, listening to Beatles music for ninety minutes before moving on to the Wreck Bar at the Castaways Motel. The next day they took a tour of Biscayne Bay on sofa tycoon Bernard Castro's yacht. A pretty fifteen-year-old local girl gained lifelong notoriety by being invited to come along. Mayor Kenneth Oka had city police escort the Beatles to the airport after their four-day stay; the disappointingly brief report that the two officers gave the mayor's daughter, Steffi Oka Freed, was that they were "dirty and smelly."

Jackie Gleason, saying he wanted to move someplace where he could play golf 365 days a year, brought a crew of 268 down by private train in 1964 to make Miami Beach the permanent home for *The Jackie Gleason Show*. Every Sunday night 40 million people watched his program, which opened with the best unpaid advertising in the world, an aerial view of the glittering Gold Coast, "the sun and fun capital of the world." There is now a Jackie Gleason Drive and a Jackie Gleason Theater of the Performing Arts. During the high holy days, at the peak of the season, the Temple Emanu-El had to move its services to the Miami Beach auditorium, where service ticket-holders stood in line beneath the "Home of the Jackie Gleason Show" sign. And in the seventies, the person who'd suggested the street dedications—the city's publicist and the man instrumental in getting these performers to come to the Beach—got his own street, Hank Meyer Boulevard. The Miss Universe and Miss USA pageants moved to the Beach in the sixties, too, but the only thing to commemorate their contribution is an amateurish panel of handprints in cement in front of a Collins Avenue hotel.

WIENER ROASTS AND LOBBY HOPPING

Most of the tourists who bought the pitches and came on down were not high rollers. They weren't renting waterfront apartments for the season or staying at the Fontainebleau; they were just typical middle-class folks from New York, Illinois, New Jersey, and Ohio. The majority were Jewish—90 percent in the wintertime, according to one estimate in the late fifties, and only a quarter to a half in the summer—and their average age was fifty-eight. They drove down and stayed for two weeks in one of the roughly 399 hotels that were not Hotel of the Year. Many of these were renovated hotels from the thirties and early forties that had made a stab at Lapidus-era luxury. The Raleigh, for instance, a seven-story Moderne tower from 1940, displayed its new, unbridled color scheme in a fifties pamphlet. The lobby was decorated with blue-green carpets, heavily patterned drapes, and purple, yellow, red, and celery furniture. One wall was painted with a mural of Queen Elizabeth knighting Walter Raleigh, while a giant TV encased in black plastic dominated another corner. The cocktail lounge had one green wall, one wall covered in red paper figured with metallic-toned musical instruments, and one mirrored wall behind a black lacquered bar. The happy expressions on the family pictured eating in the pea-green dining room look forced. Fortunately hotel management left untouched the marvelous original pool with the curlicued sides, "Florida's most beautiful," claimed the pamphlet, "as described in Look, Esquire and Cue Magazines."

If the place a tourist was staying in was fairly large, it offered the American plan, in which the guest got breakfast and dinner, maybe free cocktails and even some entertainment, for a few dollars more than the daily room rate. "It's like the Ford Falcon," said one publicist. "It isn't class, but it's what the public wants."

In 1957, ten years after it had been the Hotel of the Year, the Sherry Frontenac was offering rooms for $7 a night. Its ads included a typical week's agenda. Tuesday was practically irresistible: "Visit the solarium high atop the Sherry. Breakfast on the palm-covered patio. Calisthenics and surf-riding. Relax on your cabana chaise. Square dancing under the tropical moon to an authentic Ozark 'caller.' Fabulous Sherry dinner in the Parisian Room. Amateur nite . . . fun for everyone. Moonlight swim and wiener roast. Dance 'til?" Who could wait for Wednesday? "Early dip in the multicolored Atlantic. Poolside breakfast. Shuffleboard tournament. Prizes for all. Refreshing swim in the Sherry's Olympic salt water pool. Cocktails and social chatter. Gourmet dinner. Queen of the week . . . some lucky gal is going to be laden with wonderful prizes tonight . . . will it be you? Dancing under tropical skies to throbbing Latin rhythms."

Miami publicist Charlie Cinnamon worked as a social director at the Empress Hotel in the early fifties, where one of his daily duties was to walk around the pool area talking to guests, most of them affluent widows, in order to write the hotel newsletter—"the Yenta sheet," employees called it. Every hotel had a social director, as well as a dance instructor to teach them the mambo. "After dinner, we'd try to get them into the nightclub. But lots of times they'd just sit in the lobby, so we'd work the lobby. We had a Russian dance instructor—the more exotic the better—and he'd look around and say in a voice dripping with disdain, 'I have never seen dead people smoke.' When I was at the Sea Gull we had a radio show that would start in the lounge around 11, hosted by a disc jockey who called herself Sleepy Time Gal. She'd wear sophisticated slacks and introduce herself in a throaty voice, 'Hello, this is the Sleepy Time Gal.' She was marvelous. It was all marvelous. *Those were beautiful and sunny days.*"

Shopping, eating, cardplaying, sunbathing poolside while

In the fifties, the Americana employed sixty chefs to prepare the elaborate buffets for which Miami Beach was famous. Note the butter-sculpted seal balancing a cherry tomato.

The view from the Fontainebleau. Photographs by Henri Cartier-Bresson.

The Americana. Fox-trimmed vicuña sweaters and fur stoles were the height of fashion. Photograph by Henri Cartier-Bresson.

models in negligees from a local boutique moved among the chaise lounges, a cha-cha or mambo lesson, a makeup-instruction session, the dog or horse races or a trip to the jai-alai fronton . . . a new diversion was added to all the old Miami Beach activities—lobby-hopping. Tourists, dressed in their best crinolines, fur stoles, and plaid cummerbunds, mobbed Collins Avenue's narrow sidewalks at night, stopping by all the hotel lobbies to see who was performing there, to people watch, to check out the scene, perhaps to pinch some hotel stationery. Everyone promenaded till twelve or one o'clock, then went out for dessert at Hoffman's, Wolfie's, Dubrow's, or the Saxony's Noshery, a coffee shop that served ice-cream sundaes in vases.

"The people who came down here to vacation were northerners who'd come to this country as poor immigrants and worked hard to have some money. They didn't know anything about class. This was class," said Irma Rosenblatt.

BEACH KIDS

Residents of this small town were sophisticated enough to have such a perspective on their visitors. They were the ones who lived fifty-two weeks a year in a place gilded by wealth and sunshine and populated by gangsters, gamblers, call girls, swingers, and show-business types whose world came alive late at night. People who grew up on the Beach recognize it as a unique experience, whether they are proud of it, as most are, or have mixed feelings about the place.

"It was a very fertile environment," said Michelle Oka Doner, a New York artist who has bought an apartment in her once-again booming hometown. "I had a Russian grandfather who'd come over to my house every morning whistling like a bird, and we had a Cuban housekeeper, and then I'd go out and there would be Miami Beach spread out before me," says this sculptor whose works are inspired by the shells, rocks, and

found objects of her Beach childhood. "It was a land of abundance. My father's clients would come to the door with gifts. They'd knock and say, 'This is Mr. Tinkelman'—that was really his name—'and I have something for your father.' There'd be some Cuban cigars, a bag of grapefruits, bags of avocados, a bowl of fresh kumquats, mangoes. These things grew in people's backyards. We had a key lime tree; they only grow in a small area of southeast Florida. We'd sell key limes and lemonade, and we'd make coconut cake from fresh coconuts. At Seder dinner, when the prayer would be recited about the Jews returning someday to the Promised Land, my grandfather would interrupt and say, 'Why would anyone want to go to Jerusalem when they can go to Miami Beach?'"

"It was pristine, idyllic," said former Beachite Sandy Shapiro Friedland. "It was an island, very insulated but completely self-sufficient—there were many more businesses than there are now. You wouldn't have to go over to Miami for months. There was no industry. There were not many poor people in the school, no blacks. We were aware that we didn't have blacks, because we saw separate fountains and bathrooms in public places. We took for granted the opulence and lushness."

This mixture of old-world ties, small-town innocence, and the sophistication that came with a famous resort set Beach kids off from their peers. When Carol Unger went away to college, she was surprised to find that other teenagers did not go to nightclubs on dates. Joanne Bass's parents would take her to the Latin Quarter even on school nights. Kids were driven to school in Cadillac convertibles, and part of the fun of the summer—when the tourists left and "you could shoot a cannon down Collins Avenue (or Lincoln Road or Washington Avenue) and not hit anybody"—was sneaking into one of the empty estates along Millionaire's Row to go swimming in the rainwater that had collected in the pools. In the summer, if you weren't sent off to Blue Pine or one of the other Jewish camps in North Carolina, you'd spend the days in your family's rented cabana at one of the hotels. High-school boys whose parents owned a hotel found it handy to have a private room with a key, and the summertime activity was "cruising Collins" to pick up secretaries on vacation.

Although townies resented the tourists taking over their city nine months out of the year, hotels were integral to their social life, too. "In Miami Beach, they were the equivalent of a Kiwanis hall," said Oka Doner. "Every function was held in a hotel ballroom. I go into a grand ballroom now, and I feel right at home." Everybody had their engagement party, their wedding, their sweet-sixteen party, or their Bar Mitzvah at the Hotel of the Year, and rented a block of hotel rooms for a high-school sorority slumber party or a birthday celebration. One ornate Eden Roc wedding, between the daughter of a prominent local businessman and the son of a big hotel owner, stands out in Miami Beach social history because the groom skipped town the night before, and a then-famous stripper named Zorita acquired the dry ice, wind machine, and doves and incorporated them into her act. Another renowned occasion was Ira Hirsch's Bar Mitzvah at the Fontainebleau, when Frank Sinatra, Sammy Davis, Peter Lawford, and Elvis Presley dropped in after taping a TV special in the adjacent ballroom. Not so impressive to a hotel owner's child like Eric Jacobs, who met plenty of celebrities when they came through his family's Lord Tarleton. "Once I had my picture taken with the Lone Ranger and Tonto. Little boys all over the world would have loved that, and I got it."

All Beach kids ended up at Miami Beach High no matter which lower school they had attended. It was extremely competitive academically and consistently claimed more Merit Scholars than any other school in the country during several years in the sixties. Friedland, class of '58, had straight A's, was the president of the student council, and was fifty-fifth in a class of 458. At their twenty-fifth reunion the emcee recited some vital statistics about the class, including the fact that of its graduates, 10.6 percent were lawyers and 6 percent were doctors. Gentiles were few and far between; one popular boy from the class of '58, Demi Zacher, got nicknamed the Number One Goyim.

Many world premieres were held at the Carib Theater on Lincoln Road in the fifties and sixties. By the early 1980s Lincoln Road had become a shopping mall.

Beach High graduates form their own society. Clark Gearnter said that there is a group of guys in town in their fifties who still "get together when a friend comes in from out of town. I never hear my friends from New York and New Jersey talking about doing that." Bill Pine is a businessman in L.A. The story goes that when he was at a hospital there for the birth of his child, he was just leaning over to see the newborn when he heard over the loudspeaker, "Dr. Lockman, Dr. Norman Lockman . . . ," and Pine's head popped up. "Hey, that's Norm Lockman! He went to Beach High!"

Not everyone has such glowing memories of growing up on the Beach. Allan Albert, a theatrical producer in New York, claimed that even though "everybody's re-appreciating Miami Beach now, then we wanted out. People won't admit this, but we were embarrassed of our immigrant grandparents. Especially the smart kids. We had complicated childhoods. Many of our parents had been poor. So we had the immediacy of pov-

erty on one hand and the Holocaust on the other. Having the Holocaust as an immediate past detail is not insignificant—it makes for self-doubt and fear, but also striving and ambition. I wasn't ashamed of being Jewish, but the values of Miami Beach made me uncomfortable. You know, you went to the Pappagallo store on Lincoln Road, and you bought ten pairs of shoes and got one free. Can you imagine?" That fascination with money and what it could buy was particularly apparent to someone who didn't have as much. "Every morning when the school bus came there was a sign on our boardinghouse that said 'Rooms to Rent,' and every morning I took it down before the bus came," said Albert. "And every afternoon when the school bus dropped me off it was back up. No one ever talked about it, but it was always like that. We never had a cabana, and we never went to camp. Those were big deals. We went to South Beach, surrounded by old people."

"I hated growing up in Miami Beach," said Audrey Corwin Wright. "Hated the people here, hated the business. I hated

Each visitor to Miami's Serpentarium received his or her very own sample of cobra venom.

everything about it. I hated the way the bookies ran everything, and I hated the clubs with the naked girls, thought they were being treated like horses, with all their plumes and sequined costumes. It was so tawdry. Everything the people here did was anathema to me. I didn't want to shack around with these jerks, these big shots. They were so rude, so full of themselves, aggrandizing their position. They couldn't get enough of homes, jewelry, furs, cars, trips. Status and appearance really didn't appeal to me at all. I was brought up as an extremely wealthy kid, but I didn't want a penny. I used to buy blue jeans from Sears' farm department. My father used to say, 'What are you, Communist or something?'

"I didn't nourish and flourish here," Wright continued. "There was no nature. They kept bulldozing. . . . Of course there were times, in the morning, when you'd wake at dawn and the beach was empty and the sea was just glass, and that was beautiful, but other times I loathed it. The only thing good I can remember was taking a ride on Rosie the elephant one Sunday down Lincoln Road. It was the highlight of my life."

But most residents, like the visitors, saw the resort as luxurious, not tacky. And locals enjoyed the easygoing lifestyle that tourism inspired. In the summer, Beachites would go to their hotel cabana for lunch and a swim before going back to work. Mothers with children would stay the whole day, before there was air-conditioning. On Lincoln Road, the Carib Theater had parrots in the lobby and a roof that rolled back so you could watch the movie with the stars above you, and next to the entrance of Saks Fifth Avenue a stream of cologne was released from a little hole in the sidewalk every few minutes. "It was all so clean and nice," one woman said. "I call the fifties the Leave It to Beaver years."

Another mom remembered that a typical day was going to the Roney for lunch, a swim, and martinis, then sending the kids home in a taxi around five, with money for pizza. "Then we'd go to the clubs. Our hangout was Teddie's. It had three clubs under one roof to save on liquor licenses. The Grate was the middle bar. It served steaks, and all the good jazz people

would perform there. South of this bar was the Pin-Up, a hangout for all the local lesbians and gays. The north-end bar was the Night Owl, a long narrow room—one person could sit at the bar and the other squeeze in behind. It had a jukebox that only played Frank Sinatra records that the bartender fed. All night long we'd wander from one bar to the next, meeting all our friends. The place reeked of marijuana. Cops hung out there, and Sinatra and Sammy Davis, Jr.—all the entertainers and showgirls would go there after their performances. Everybody was a jazz fanatic and everybody drank a lot and stayed out till five a.m."

Miami Beach was a late-night town, and even the Leave It to Beaver set stayed out till two, noshing at Wolfie's. You could start the evening at five, going to one of the hotel lounges for Latin music ("Pupi Campo was very popular—big sleeves and *very* tight crotch—he taught Tom Jones what to do with it"). Then there was dinner, at the Embers or the Park Avenue, followed by a show at one of the big nightclubs—Ciro's, the Latin Quarter, Copa City, the Beachcomber—that played the top acts like Tony Bennett, Sophie Tucker, and Betty Hutton.

Vacationland, USA: 1954–1969

Miami Beach was also a place where up-and-coming entertainers—comedians, singers, musicians—were scouted during the winter season, performing at the nightclubs on and around Dade Boulevard. When radio talk-show host Larry King first came to Miami in the late fifties, he wrote in his memoir *Tell It to the King*, he broadcast his radio show from Pumpernick's delicatessen. The Beach was such a hopping place then that all he had to do was sit there and collar some of the famous people that came through.

Michael Gatti worked in his family's popular restaurant, Gatti's, which his grandfather opened across from the Flamingo Hotel in the twenties. A stream of celebrities and crooks ate there, Gatti remembered. "Jackie Gleason was great publicity for us—he'd come in here two nights a week. When Shirley MacLaine was dating Sander Vanocur they used to sit in the front room and have violent arguments. Arthur Godfrey would come in, and we'd make a special dish for him—calves liver with raisins marinated in cognac and white wine." The restaurant was also a hotbed for the Teamsters—Jimmy Hoffa came in often, and "Meyer Lansky and his cronies were cus-

ABOVE: *Debbie Reynolds and fiancé, Eddie Fisher, in Miami Beach, 1955.*

OPPOSITE: *Desi Arnaz (right) with Murray Franklin at Franklin's nightclub. Visitors to the men's room were serenaded by a pianist.*

RIGHT: *Jake La Motta and his former wife, Vicky, at his Collins Avenue nightclub.*

tomers for fifty years. I was always astonished by how many perfectly legitimate people used to know them. J. Edgar Hoover used to come in—he was a buddy of both Dad and Granddad. I remember one night in the sixties—I'm sure there were many nights like this—where Hoover was at table three, Lansky was at four, and John Knight, who owned a newspaper chain, was at fifteen."

After-hours, the hip crowd went to Overtown to hear jazz greats like Miles Davis and Ramsey Lewis at the Sir John Hotel, or to North Bay Village, a small town strung out on the Seventy-ninth Street causeway between the Beach and Miami. Lounges there were allowed to stay open till 7 a.m. The "players"—the gangsters, gamblers, playboys, and sports people— hung out at Radio Winer's Bonfire; even Howard Hughes, who had a house on the Beach in the fifties, would sometimes show up, parking his beat-up Chevy two blocks away. The Bonfire restaurant, whose specialty was that foot-high chocolate cake, sat six hundred; the lounge had a piano-shaped bar that could seat fifty, with a stage in the middle of it for jazz trios. There were always plenty of hookers hanging around— but "nice hookers," one man pointed out. A Place for Steak, owned by a small-time hoodlum known as Lefty Clark, was another favorite. "In the early fifties, that part of town wasn't built up yet," remembered a former habitué. "Looking out east, there was nothing between you and the Atlantic Ocean. You could sit at the bar with a drink in your hand and watch the sun come up. It was beautiful."

But the high local color was fading, flattening. As the number of hotel rooms ballooned and the competition for tourist dollars became more fierce, individual hotels swallowed up many of the service and entertainment functions that had made the city lively. The package plan became the order of the day, and the packages became more and more generous. Whereas once it had been the sophisticated urbanite who came to Miami Beach, now the middle classes crowded into the hotels. "Class versus Mass" was a phrase developers had liked to use when

discussing the city's future, but it was a dead argument. Hotels were happy just to keep their rooms filled.

Despite the promotional rhetoric, the city *was* overdeveloped, at least as far as tourism was concerned. At one point in the forties, the demand for hotel rooms was greater than the supply. But by the time the Fontainebleau was opened, the city was saturated with hotels, and more were abuilding. The Fontainebleau and other big hotels began to operate as resort worlds that the tourist never needed to leave, and their monopolies had a ripple effect in the community. Small hotels that couldn't afford to offer meals to their guests on the American plan felt the pinch, independent restaurants weren't getting their share of the business, and the shopping arcades in some hotels drained customers from the stores on Collins Avenue and Lincoln Road. The city commissioned Morris Lapidus to transform the former Rue de la Paix of Miami Beach into a pedestrian mall in a well-intentioned but unsuccessful attempt to attract customers.

The entertainment scene was a conspicuous casualty of the hotel warfare. Some hotels had always had a singer or a comic or a modest floor show, but when the Fontainebleau opened, it included its own supper club offering the kind of top-flight entertainers—Frank Sinatra, Jerry Lewis, Liberace—that appeared only at the best Beach nightclubs. Then all of the big hotels began to book name headliners, and since they were able to pay them higher salaries than the clubs could, the clubs were slowly forced out of business. Hotels weren't the nightclubs' only enemy; television was also making them obsolete by offering both stars and newcomers much more money and public exposure for much less work. As the typical tourist bankroll got smaller and the hotels more anxious for business, they began to offer the shows to guests for free, and to sell seats to nightclub bus tours for fixed rates, throwing in a free midnight snack. Maître d's called the tour-bus guests the chicken-sandwich crowd. The glitter set had moved on.

Paul Bruun edited a weekly newspaper called the Miami Beach *Reporter*, famous for its freewheeling editorial column,

"Bruun Over Miami." Here is one from 1963 written in his singular style, in which he blasts his favorite target, Miami Beach politicians, for the city's waning fortunes.

There was a time when this area abounded in sophisticated night clubs. (I should have owned my own paper then.) Think of the glory that was Lou Walter's Latin Quarter. (Lou is now at the Carillon with the exact same elaborate type revue.) Remember Copa City, of which there was none more elegant anywhere on the face of the earth? Remember the Beachcomber, the Five O'Clock Club, Ciro's? The Brook Club is now a supermarket. Publix Markets is building where Gray's Inn was.

The fabulous Park Avenue is now a library parking lot. What was the famous Hickory House is a garage. The Clover Club in Miami is a vacant lot. Papa Bouche used to be able to present his unique revue to a paying audience. I don't remember a single one of these places ever closing immediately after Jan. 1, and staying closed most of January. . . .

All around us in the islands that are expanding their hotel facilities, like the $30,000,000.00 in new hotels of which Puerto Rico currently boasts for this year, there are casinos. Remember when hotel owners formerly damned "Bruun Over Miami" because he boosted the shows and casinos in Havana? Now that Castro Castro'd them, these same hotel owners blame part of their loss of business on the absence today of the fun that was but a few minutes away from Miami Beach.

In Las Vegas, in all the islands like Aruba, etc., there are casinos to pay the high prices demanded by name bands and stars. In Miami Beach night club impresarios are supposed to compete in this high salaried field with "profits" from the sale of meat, potatoes and drinks. It can't be done. ALL the entertainment in the hotel costs is SUBSIDIZED by room rents. . . .

With our town so very clean today, WHY aren't our hotels and our restaurants and our Miami Beach shops filled to overflowing??? Not a single person has the guts to call them as they are except Paul M. Bruun.

Believe me, friends, I would rather see vacationers with their bellies massaging crap tables, than no tourists at all. I would rather see customers in strip and burlesque clubs than no customers at all. Everybody is taking away from our town. WHO is there to put in place those things that are proven attractions for tourists? Nothing has yet been devised that compares with a crap table.

Sunshine is wonderful. We have it. Today, sunshine has been proven inadequate. Don't tell me Miami Beach NEEDS more advertising and publicity. NUTS!!!!

With President Kennedy basking in SUNSHINE two days during the past week in the Orange Bowl, with the eyes of the continent upon him, and with blizzards killing people in the north, again I say SUNSHINE HERE AND BLIZZARDS THERE aren't the answer today.

Most everybody in Greater Miami Beach is content to bury his head in the sand of doing nothing. Leadership is sadly lacking.

There was no new Hotel of the Year in 1960, despite a record two and a half million tourists that season. Rate cutting was the order of the day—prices had dropped as much as 25 percent in just five years as hotels competed against each other. Some hotels worked with the airlines, selling blocks of rooms at a discount to tour groups and conventions.

More than twenty-five hotels were in trouble, and four well-known ones had declared bankruptcy. It wasn't the first time that had happened. The Biltmore Terrace had been auctioned in 1954, only three years old and with a string of claimants against it.

Since the war, hotel buying and selling had become a big financial game, played largely by inexperienced investors lured by the prospect of easy profits. During the good years of the boom, a luxury hotel could make about 15 to 25 percent profit per year, earning the initial investment back in a few years. That was the simplest equation. Hotel owners routinely elaborated upon it in order to skim money from hotel profits by manipulating various leasing arrangements. The service function of the business took a lower priority, and as the financing became more complicated, less money was available to put back into hotel maintenance and improvements. A rule of thumb was that a luxury hotel ceased to be one within about five years of its construction.

One corporation, or syndicate, for instance, might have gotten a ninety-nine-year lease on a piece of property for low annual payments. The corporation would build a hotel, make some money, then form another corporation, which it controlled, and sublease the property to them for double the amount they paid. The larger amount would be drawn from the hotel profits, the original amount paid to the landowner, and the surplus divided among the members of the corporation.

The lease itself was valuable and could be used as collateral to get a bank loan. If the lease was mortgaged in order to give the corporation money for another investment, the hotel profits had to cover the payment of the lease, the mortgage payments, and the interest.

The corporation that built the hotel usually piled up mortgages—the first might be given to a bank, an insurance company, or a closed investment trust; a second mortgage to a construction company in lieu of payment; a third in exchange for operating capital. Hotels were known to have acquired up to fourteen mortgages—the number that Ben Novack's Fontainebleau had when it went into foreclosure in 1976—each mortgage holder with a claim upon the assets.

The hotel corporation might also lease the building to a second corporation that it controlled, which would then sublease it to an operating corporation, which would pay, say, $1,500 per room per year. The operating corporation could then sublease again to someone else for $1,800 per room per year. And this subleasor could sublease, and so on.

"There's a lot of smart money out on the Beach," one real-estate man said at the time. "Too smart for me."

If existing hotels didn't have enough problems, a zoning change in 1957 allowed hotels and apartment buildings to be built along Millionaire's Row from the Fontainebleau north to the city limits. In the early sixties, several fourteen-story apartment complexes went up, with their own beaches, parking garages, swimming pools, social rooms, sometimes even shops. Now the big hotels were in pain because the kind of people who used to stay with them were renting apartments for the season or even moving down permanently.

The biggest hotels could at least set their sights on continued patronage through convention business—the Miami area was now one of the top four convention sites in the country—but it was clear that there wasn't going to be an ever-increasing supply of tourists. Although by the mid-sixties the Beach was still the single most popular tourist destination in the country, more visitors came in the summer now, when deals were cheaper and conventions more plentiful.

The Beach was taking on a harder edge as things tightened up—the action more frenetic, the search for a good time a lit-tle more desperate. The city was portrayed as a place full of confidence men and gold diggers, everyone pretending to be someone or something they weren't. A *Saturday Evening Post* article told the story of a guy trying to pick up a girl by telling her he'd gone to Yale, just lost $50,000 in a card game, etcetera. But she balked when, at the end of the night, she discovered he was staying in a second-class hotel. "'What could I do?' he said. 'I told her the place was just enough of a dump to be sophisticated, like a foreign movie, but she said her mother told her never to go out with men who didn't stay at the Eden Roc.'"

The sixties was a moment when all the eras of Miami Beach overlapped. Musicians were still working who had backed Sophie Tucker and could perform requests for "I Wish I Could Shimmy Like My Sister Kate," while Harry Belafonte and Joey Bishop played the Eden Roc and Totie Fields starred in "You Gotta Have Mazel" at the Lucerne Hotel. The posh old night-clubs were on the verge of being turned into bowling alleys; now there were strip joints and discotheques, such as the Wreck bar at the Castaways, featuring the Maad, Maad Maids

OPPOSITE: *By the late fifties, upper Collins Avenue was packed with hotels, but development stopped at the Eden Roc (see top of picture). Massive apartment buildings would soon fill in the land north of there, once lined with mansions.*

Miami Beach, 1966. One women's magazine said the city was "ideally, a three-bathing-suit town."

The Life and Times of Miami Beach

The Fleur de Lys Room of the Fontainebleau. Louis XIV in papier-mâché presided over the diners. At the Mona Lisa Pavilion of the Eden Roc next door, the walls were lined with reproductions of famous paintings.

A-Go-Go, or Caesar's Forum—"modeled on Hadrian's villa"—a four-story houseboat moored on Indian Creek that had been turned into a floating nightclub. In the declining days of the Miami Beach style, it came complete with a fountain, reflecting pool, and marble floors, diamond-tufted chairs, nude torsos, and "statues of Grecian revels." In the dining room, food was delivered in little chariots; the tabletops were modeled after Roman coins. A frieze at the entrance depicted the owner's life, from his birth in Brooklyn to his success in the tile business.

The influx of Cuban refugees that had flooded Miami since Castro's 1958 coup took a special twist in Miami Beach. Twenty thousand Jews had been living in Cuba at the time, most of them Russian and Eastern European natives; they had

temporarily settled on the island in the teens and twenties as they waited to be allowed to enter the United States, and then decided to stay when they found little religious persecution in Cuba. But between 1959 and 1963, all but about a thousand of them migrated, 90 percent of them to Miami Beach. The Ashkenazi settled south of Lincoln Road, concentrating around Sixteenth and Pennsylvania. They built their first synagogue on Seventeenth and Michigan, the conservative Temple Beth Shmuel, or the Cuban Hebrew Congregation. The Sephardic Jews moved to the northern end of the Beach and established an orthodox temple, Temple Moses, on Normandy Drive.

They were the latest generation of Jewish immigrants to find their Promised Land in Miami Beach. The original settlement of Eastern European Jews who had come to the Beach as tourists in the thirties had grown old in South Beach, although there were still elderly new recruits from northern cities to keep the little South Beach hotels constantly occupied. Occasionally a tourist on a roll would blunder into the world of tiny South Beach hotels inhabited by the aged. "You vant a room with fresh towels?" Michelle Oka Doner would hear her grandfather sometimes say from behind the desk at his Neptune Hotel. "Uh-huh . . . you vant a room with an ocean view? . . . Un-huh . . . you vant a room with twenty-four-hour room service? Yeah? So get outta here!"

While old men sat on the benches at Lummus Park, singing in Yiddish and playing mandolins, Miami Beach socialites lunched at the Surf Club in hot-pink Pucci stretch pants, and Bath Club members watched their daughters model clothes from the Miss Teenage Snob Shop. Poolside cha-cha lessons were out; the hully-gully was in. Lenny Bruce rented a room in one of the old South Beach hotels and turned it into his personal nightclub. The Roney was still open in 1965, welcoming guests who had been coming there for decades; the following year Carl Fisher's former wife, Jane, wearing a hard hat, officiated at its demolition, and a monolithic, block-long apartment building went up on the site. Meyer Lansky and his

brother had moved back to the area ("Just what I need," thought former police chief Rocky Pomerance when the FBI called to give him the news, "a *high-profile* creep"), Lansky maintaining interests in hundreds of hotels and motels in and around Miami Beach. He was often seen walking his dog or having dinner with friends, a little guy in droopy pants, whose only bodyguard looked about eighty years old. But he controlled a web of criminal activity—in jukeboxes, hotels, motels, laundry services, and the like—in and around the city. "Miami Beach isn't controlled by the mob," said its mayor at the time, Elliott Roosevelt. "It's run by the mob."

"Miami was the end of the world," wrote Miami *Herald* crime reporter Edna Buchanan in *The Corpse Had a Familiar Face.* "The last stop for sun-seeking drifters and people on the run from trouble." Murf the Surf performed stunt-diving routines at hotel pools—"just another creep," said Pomerance, until Murf merged with a bright criminal attorney and a high-powered fence. He was later convicted of the theft of the Star of India, and once out, murdered two young women on Miami Beach and threw them into Indian Creek waterway, where they promptly floated to the top.

Usually the crimes and the criminals were less violent. If *Miami Vice* had been shot here then, the plotlines would have involved scams rather than drugs. The Beach was a community of wealthy people and the people who preyed on them; Miami Beach, along with cities like Beverly Hills, Palm Beach, and Saratoga, was on their circuit. Miami Beach may have been particularly vulnerable. "We're fickle," said one longtime resident. "If you're flashy, it doesn't matter that you've just blown into town."

Sometimes the scam was big time and sometimes it was just selling merchandise to tourists that was supposed to be hot, but was simply cheap.

The last new luxury hotel to go up on Miami Beach was a Hilton in 1967, a burgundy-and-blue-velvet affair that made a valiant effort to "bring back the poshness to Miami Beach."

Jackie Gleason was hired as the hotel's creative consultant, lending his name and image to the Jackie Gleason Bon Vivant Room, the Joe the Bartender bar, and Jackie Gleason's Great Room. Other hotel operators charged that this was unfair competition, but the uproar was settled at a Jackie Gleason Appreciation luncheon: Gleason sat on a throne while rival hoteliers came up to pay homage. It didn't make much difference, anyway; the hotel changed hands, and names, several times in the next ten years.

The Beach had victimized itself by overbuilding, overfinancing, and making its beach impassible. But other forces were beyond its control. Jet travel made other destinations as easily and quickly accessible as Florida, and many preferred the unspoiled Caribbean or the prestige of a European vacation. It just wasn't enough anymore to come home with a wet bathing suit in your luggage.

On top of everything else, the materialistic lifestyle that Miami Beach was designed to celebrate had simply gone out of fashion. Sometimes it seemed like Miami Beach was glitz's last refuge.

"I was going to Beach High in the sixties," one Beach kid remembered. "The world was in turmoil—and the parking lot at school was full of red Corvette convertibles. All I wanted was to move to Boston."

OPPOSITE: *In the sixties, the Wreck Bar at the Castaways Motel in Sunny Isles was the swingingest club in town.*

LEFT: *When in Miami Beach, Lenny Bruce used to rent his own nightclub room in a run-down South Beach hotel and perform there.*

BELOW: *Meyer Lansky living the life of any elderly Miami Beachite. It was said that residents of the Imperial House, the luxury apartment building on Collins Avenue where Lansky lived, never needed to take out homeowner's insurance.*

HOTEL OWNERS

Miami Beach has been built by and on characters. Some were local personalities like the man who marched up and down the beach in leopard shoes and a white suit with a red carnation in the lapel. Or Silver Dollar Jake, who drove around the Beach in a red convertible, tossing silver dollars to schoolchildren, and was sometimes hired to appear at birthday parties. There were a number of exiled princesses, of possibly even more questionable authenticity than the ones who settled in Palm Beach; one opened a ballet school, another lived off air and drove around in a car missing the driver's-side door. And then there were the scam artists of various degrees of audacity who drifted into town. Many were simply "third children," as Michelle Oka Doner called them, bad boys who couldn't make it up north and came down to live the high life while running up debts and accumulating mortgages.

But the monumental characters, everyone agrees, were the hotel owners who reached the peaks of their success in the forties and fifties. "They were gutter fighters," said architect Alan Lapidus, Morris Lapidus's son. "They clawed their way up to the American Dream. The banks didn't finance these places. Many made money in the black market during the war. They invented their own kingdom in Miami Beach, and they succeeded so well because they only had to deal with a limited audience." Morris Lapidus, like other people who were contracted to work for them, had a harsher assessment. "They were monsters," he said. "I might as well say it; they're almost all dead now. The exception for me were the Tisches, who hired me to build the Americana."

"Everybody who came here had a driving, domineering personality," said Audrey Corwin Wright. "They *had* to be extroverts to come down with a few bucks and scrounge around until they jockeyed to make a deal, to swing it on credit or their looks or by sleeping with someone. The people that came down made it work because they were willing to throw themselves into it 100 percent.

"I was a terrible anti-Semite growing up here then, but when I look back now I have to admire the integrity of the people. They were brave, bold, and had a sense of pride and accomplishment. They pulled themselves out of the gutter and established a permanence for their children."

Gender didn't matter if one was sufficiently scrappy. Wright's grandmother, Katie Pollack, left a millinery business in Chicago to come to Florida in the twenties for her son's health and, starting with one South Beach apartment building, built a hotel dynasty. "She was clever," said Pollack's daughter Bea Courshon. "She knew how to play on people. I remember once we were sitting around the Belmar pool and some people came up to talk to her, old people, and she complimented them on looking so good. And I said, 'How can you say they look good when they look terrible?' 'Does it cost me anything?' she said." Pollack's chutzpah was passed on to another daughter, businesswoman Muriel "the Hat" Anis Hirsch Pick, who schemed with the best of them. "She took a fabulous personal posture," said Wright, Pick's daughter. "It was 'I can do no wrong, I can't make a mistake.' When I was taking care of her affairs I found out lots. But she never let a person know, they never heard of a business deal that went off bad or where she was taken or robbed or broke. But it happened. She was smart. Why should she tell? It was showing your vulnerability. She got everything she wanted, everything—minks, furs, sables, emeralds, diamonds, Rolls-Royces, chauffeurs, boats. She aggrandized it, but my mother did make a tremendous amount of money." Then there was Polly de Hirsch Meyer, a former Ziegfeld Follies showgirl who became a contractor and hotel owner in the forties, the wife of Baron (his first name) de Hirsch Meyer, who built his own fortune starting with South Beach hotels. Polly later became a prominent racehorse owner, and, according to local wags, took to signing into European hotels as the Baronness de Hirsch Meyer.

Although it seemed almost everyone was in hotels, or closely connected to them, by the fifties a few names dominated the business—Sam Mufson, Sam Cohen, Morris Lansburgh, J. Meyer Schine, and Ben Novack.

The people who worked for these hotelmen remember them for their eccentric, to say the least, business practices. When architect Mel Grossman rode the elevator with his boss, Sam Cohen, up to his office, Cohen would stop floor by floor to check room-service carts left in the hallway, and he'd pocket any leftover sugar packets. Seymour Gerber, a graphic designer for many Beach hotels and motels in the fifties and sixties, was told by Alvin Kascell, the owner of the Carillon ("It didn't really have anything to do with a bell tower," said Gerber), that he could make the logo any color he wanted as long as it was green.

"They were ghastly people," said interior decorator Henry End. "Only a few had any experience running a hotel." Many hotel owners routinely cut deals with purveyors (the kickback system). "Milking, I always heard my father talk about milking this or that," one hotel owner's daughter mused. They were also reputed to cheat the people contracted to work for them—at the least, they made them miserable. End had a five-year contract in the fifties with J. Meyer Schine, whose son David was Roy Cohn's protégé during the House Un-American Activities hearings. Among Schine's holdings was the Roney Plaza, the grande dame of Beach hotels, yet despite his many millions, Schine wasn't making his monthly payments to End. The decorator went to see him and told him he was having trouble paying his bills. "Here's what I can do," said Schine in a businesslike way. "We can pay you half what we owe you now or you can sue me for the full amount." On another occasion, End found that although he had signed a contract with the owner to do the interiors on his new hotel, the job was given to a contract company. End went to court, but the owner denied having ever seen or signed the contract the designer presented, and End lost. Contractors had their own problems. One, known for being as tough as his employ-

ers, was rumored to have a printing press in his back room on which he printed phony invoices from manufacturers that he presented to hotel owners. "I screw them before they screw me," he explained to End.

Morris Lansburgh owned or had interests in the Deauville, Casablanca, Sherry Frontenac, Sans Souci, Versailles, and Crown hotels. Harold Mehling came to interview him in the sixties for his book on Miami Beach, *The Most of Everything*. "I've changed Miami Beach," Lansburgh barked as soon as Mehling sat down. "That's the story." Other people agree that in the postwar building boom he led the way in operating hotels for the mass (as opposed to the "class") market. "Morris, unfortunately, introduced the American plan to the Beach," said Eric Jacobs, whose own family ran Beach hotels since the twenties.

Lansburgh came down in the late thirties for relief from his hay fever and asthma and discovered the Beach's many money-making charms. He bought a small hotel in South Beach, then drummed up business for it by leasing "stoplight rights" along two highways in north Florida from scamming local officials. His boys positioned themselves at the stoplights and pressed a button that turned the light red whenever southbound cars approached. Then they ran out to the tourists' cars and pressed brochures for Lansburgh's hotels on them. When the tourists arrived in South Beach, bellhops from the hotel would be standing out on the street waving people inside.

But Ben Novack was clearly the most notable and outrageous of this crew. Novack came down during the Second World War and leased the Atlantis Hotel. "He knew some money people when he came," said Levenson. "And somehow that hotel, the Atlantis, was never taken over during the war and he operated it very successfully." Afterward, Novack built the Sans Souci with Harry Mufson. The Sans Souci was at the time one of the big three hotels, along with the Roney Plaza and the Saxony. Mufson, called "Gentleman Harry" (by those who liked him), was already the owner of a chain of discount stores, but he enjoyed the social nature of hotels. Novack took

During the sixties, Frank Sinatra was a fixture at the
Fontainebleau. Here with his bodyguards. Photograph by
Terry O'Neill.

care of the administrative duties, and Mufson was the front man, greeting the guests, juggling their room requests, stroking their vanity. Jealousies developed between the two men, and Novack devised his grand plan for the Fontainebleau, an audacious move that made him the premier hotelman on the Beach.

"People told Novack he was crazy to build a hotel so far from Lincoln Road, which was the hub of the city," said Novack's former publicist Hal Gardner. "But the men who built Miami Beach were motivated by the spirit of the adventurers of old. They were opening new horizons. Miami Beach had nothing to offer without their planting the seeds of success."

"Ben Novack was an absolutely amazing man," said Charlie Cinnamon. "They should have made a movie about this man. Courageous . . . he had vision. Who else would have built the Fontainebleau? It's a monumental achievement."

Novack reveled in his position and did his best to squash any competition. When Mufson used Lapidus as well to build the Eden Roc, next door to the Fontainebleau, Novack built a new wing to his hotel, not for the extra rooms—"Ben was not a marketing guy," said Jacobs—but to serve as a spite wall that blocked the sun over the Eden Roc's pool for most of the day. The back of the wing was an almost unbroken wall of concrete; one window marking Novack's private suite of rooms pierced the upper-left corner, where he looked down on his neighbor and thumbed his nose.

Another long-running feud was carried on with the Miami *Herald*, which published a series of articles in the early seventies investigating the hotelman's alleged link to the mob. The paper claimed that the Fontainebleau's original group of backers included several members of the Minneapolis combine. At the end of a libel suit against the paper, the *Herald* reported that an insurance company held the title to the land and that Novack was sole owner of the operating company. Novack had the article framed and mounted in his office. Not that mobsters were exactly unwelcome at the hotel. "Oh, sure," said a former Fontainebleau carhop. "I used to park Charlie Fischetti's car all the time—'Mr. Fish,' we used to call him. He was always yelling at Novack." Novack also took umbrage with Charles Kimball, the coauthor of the *Herald* series, when he later reported that the Fontainebleau was in foreclosure, a matter of public record. Novack denied it and sent Kimball a letter calling him a "dirty grasshopper."

Miami Beach, Decline and Resurrection: 1970 to the Present

It's a city trapped in time, an American Pompeii.
—Miami Beach tourist, 1988

Well-to-do senior citizens, many of them former tourists in the sixties, abandoned the hotels for their own condominiums in the high rises built on upper Collins Avenue. Some condos had shops, twenty-four-hour medical services— even nightclubs.

The seventies and early eighties were bad years for the Beach. The country's recession and the resort's flagging popularity dovetailed disastrously. The city invested large amounts of municipal funds in order to host the 1968 Republican convention, and both the Republican and Democratic 1972 conventions. (Presidential tapes played during the Watergate investigation revealed Richard Nixon agreeing to hold the convention at "that stupid damn place" again.) City officials welcomed the national coverage Miami Beach received during the weeks surrounding the events, even if much of it was snide. (An "Everyman's Eden," *Newsweek* called it, ". . . that offered immediate asylum from the tyranny of tastemakers, cultural commissars and other bluenoses.") But no one got rich off the conventions, and the coverage didn't help lure back tourists.

The swinging Beach was seen to be suffering from old age, in many ways. The average Miami Beach citizen was sixty-six by 1972, ten years older than the 1960 average and the highest in the country. Many of the children who had grown up there had moved to Coconut Grove to start their own families because the Beach was too expensive for them. By the mid-seventies South Beach Elementary school had closed, and the maternity ward at Mt. Sinai hospital had been scaled back. The hotels were not wearing well, some because they were old, most because hoteliers had been busy taking money out of operations, not putting it back into improvements. And the city did little to force hotels to at least maintain a spruce exterior. As a result, the clientele of the hotels and rental apartments began to match the property.

The number of tourists had sharply declined, as had their

spending power. It had always been true that the older the hotel, the less affluent its clientele. But a quality bell curve had always been maintained. Now even the Fontaine-bleau, the standard-bearer of deluxe, wasn't keeping up appearances. "The last time we went to the Beach must have been in the mid-seventies," said Lillian Meckler, a former tourist whose family yearly made the trek from Detroit. "We walked into the Fontainebleau and they had a car in the lobby. I almost cried." Promotions poolside, yes; but not among the classy statuary and jazzy marble floors.

If there was one aspect of the city that seemed to epitomize the Beach's problems, it was South Beach. The Depression-era hotels along lower Collins Avenue and the ocean had been left behind in the postwar boom. Retirees had frequented the neighborhood's little apartment buildings since they were built in the thirties, and many had gradually been turned into retirement hotels.

Almost half of Miami Beach's population lived south of Lincoln Road by 1970—more than 40,000 people. Eighty percent of them were sixty-five or over, and 85 percent were Jewish, remnants of the wave of immigration from Eastern Europe at the turn of the century. There were almost 20,000 Russian Jews alone. Miami Beach was the last stop on a trip that had taken them first to New York's Lower East Side, then to

Brooklyn or the Bronx. Yiddish was the unofficial language of South Beach, and some people even made a living writing letters in English to the sons and daughters up north who never learned the old language. Merchants and politicians wisely advertised in Yiddish, but the city didn't recognize it. After jaywalkers caused several traffic accidents on Washington Avenue, the heart of the Jewish neighborhood, a citizens' committee decided to post "No Jaywalking" signs in English and Spanish. Sometime later a police officer stopped an old man jaywalking. "Hey," said the cop, "didn't you see the sign?" "So who's smoking?" said the old man.

Many of these South Beachers first came down on vacation in the thirties and forties, and had a long association with the city. Others might have joined sons or daughters who moved there after the Second World War, or simply made their way down on the advice of neighbors. Over the years, the retirees' small fixed incomes were decimated by inflation, rising rents, health problems, and widowhood, bringing their standard of living to the poverty level. Some survived on $28 a week. On the days the banks figured interest on accounts, oldsters stood in line to withdraw the extra bit of money.

A 1974 book called *Dying in the Sun*, by Donn Pearce, described the illness and destitution that permeated this community. The reports of the South Beach rescue crew, which may have answered thirty emergency calls on a peak day in the winter season, were "a litany of senility," wrote Pearce. "'Subject complained of being nauseated. Age eighty.' 'Subject was sleeping. Roommate said she complained of colon trouble. Age ninety-three.' 'Subject was lying on floor. Small cut on foot from broken glass tabletop. Belts tied together. Apparent suicide attempt. Moaning and screaming. Had apparently slipped out of noose. Age seventy-four.' 'Blood pressure 210/100. Abdominal pain. Age eighty-one.' 'Subject complained of pain in her chest. Age seventy-eight.' 'Subject took sleeping pill and didn't know it. Couldn't stay awake. Had thimble still on her finger as sleeping.'"

By 1980, South Beach was the poorest neighborhood per capita in the state. Yet the community had attractions that still managed to attract a steady stream of lonely pensioners. It offered a community of peers and an independent living situation—often a small hotel room converted, with the addition of a stove and sink, into what was locally called a "pullmanette." South Beach was also a pedestrian-friendly neighborhood where prescriptions could be filled, cigar supplies replenished, and city council meetings attended within walking distance of home. There were seven synagogues, as well as churches, in the neighborhood, and some of the hotels held religious services in former meeting rooms and nightclubs. For those who were able, the Beach offered a rich social life. Musicales and dances were held at the pier, and there were political rallies at a city-designated Friendship Corner in Lummus Park. Many of the elderly had worked in the garment industry, and men who had been among the original trade unionists of the twenties debated radical politics in Flamingo Park. Although women outnumbered men by two to one, there was plenty of sex and many remarriages. Two writers for the Miami Beach *Reporter* published a popular book in 1968 called *Sex and the Senior Citizen* that covered, in oversize type, topics like sex and Social Security, gigolos and gold diggers, finding love in retirement hotels, and the estrogen pill. The book even included recipes for stuffed cabbage, kugel, and tzimmes, to warm the heart of the lonely widower.

Despite its poverty, South Beach was thus a vibrant neighborhood, but that was not the perception of the public. Varicose Beach, Senile City, the Elephants' Graveyard, God's Waiting Room, Mausoleum in the Sun, it was variously called. Newness, the Beach's lifeblood, was in short supply. So when there was no more oceanfront property to develop, all eyes turned to South Beach. The drab little beige hotels and chunky apartment buildings clustered there seemed eminently dispensable.

In the mid-seventies, the city hoped to resuscitate the Beach's reputation through an elaborate redevelopment project for a portion of South Beach, the 250 acres at the tip of the

island, from Government Cut to Sixth Street. All except a few buildings, such as Joe's Stone Crab, would have been razed, the old streets abandoned for new ones. Sketches showed water taxis plying a network of canals, carrying conventioneers from the lobbies of nine new hotels to the door of a new convention center. Included in the plan were nearly half a million square feet of entertainment and retail space, offices, 3,300 residential units, including some housing for the elderly already living in the area, a marina, a water world, an environmental world, and a sea habitat.

It looked great—in theory. But there were problems. One was that the area, at the tip of South Beach, was inhabited by more than 5,000 people, most of them elderly, some of them Holocaust survivors, and as one observer said, "You don't tell people with a number tattooed on their arm that they have to relocate." There were years of public hearings, with arguments centering on whether the area was truly a slum in need of redevelopment and with activist senior citizens demanding that any relocation housing be permanently designated for the elderly. As negotiations dragged on, interest rates hit record highs and the development authority was unable to persuade builders to

The Ninth Street Friendship Corner was a gathering place for the Eastern European Jews of South Beach.

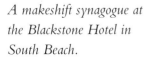

A makeshift synagogue at the Blackstone Hotel in South Beach.

invest in the project. It was finally abandoned in 1981.

The South Shore project did not go gently. The city had imposed a building moratorium on the neighborhood as the plan was being formulated, and home and hotel owners were not allowed to do more than minor repairs on their aging structures. By the time the moratorium was lifted in 1983, many residents had moved out or had been forced to let their properties fall into serious disrepair, and property values had sunk. When the Mariel boatlift brought 125,000 Cubans to South Florida in 1980, many found cheap housing in run-down South Beach. Poverty bred street crime and drug traffic in what had once been a safe and friendly, if shabby, neighborhood.

As the South Shore plan floundered, the city turned to what looked like the magic bullet of aging resorts: legalized gambling. A statewide referendum was called in 1978 to legalize casino gambling for a twenty-mile-long strip of the Gold Coast, from Miami Beach north. But the opposition was too great: Florida's Governor Reubin Askew was against it, Miami law authorities pointed out that organized crime was already the biggest growth industry in the area, and the owners of the pari-mutuel horse and dogtracks and jai-alai frontons, fearing the competition from casinos, lobbied against it. Hotel owners tried once again in 1986; this time state residents voted on a proposal to give each county—Miami Beach drew up plans to become its own county—the option to legalize casinos at hotels with five hundred rooms or more. But this was also defeated, as was a recent referendum.

RESTORATION

By the 1980s, the name Miami Beach had become a terrible irony: except at Lummus Park, there hardly was a beach, and the shoreline had become a worst-case scenario for beach

The Army Corps of Engineers had first proposed restoring the beach in the sixties, but hotel owners who had beachfront rights resisted because it would have meant making the beach public. It took more than ten years for the project to be approved. The restoration was completed in 1982.

The early days of the Art Deco–preservation movement. Developers won the battle over the New Yorker Hotel, pictured here. It was demolished in 1981.

preservationists. To bolster the city's tourism base and to protect the buildings against storms and hurricanes, the Army Corps of Engineers began an enormous beach-replenishment project. The dredge, the "national emblem of Florida," as Will Rogers had called it in the twenties, was back again, scooping up the ocean bottom and piping up tons of sand to the shore. By 1982, Miami Beach and communities to the north had acquired 10.5 miles of new beach, with an average width of 250 feet. Lummus Park was over 300 feet deep, prompting criticism that the elderly could no longer reach the water. A storm-protecting sand dune 20 feet wide and 2½ feet high rimmed the shore. It was the biggest beach-restoration project ever completed.

As the redevelopment plan was being debated in the mid-seventies a design writer and publicist named Barbara Baer Capitman and an interior designer named Leonard Horowitz, both antidevelopment environmentalists, decided to make a tour of Miami, "looking for a cause," admitted Horowitz, to illustrate their think-small philosophy. They discovered South Beach, which interested them both for its architecture, whose style they then knew very little about, and its elderly population. They and a group of followers surveyed the buildings of South Beach and submitted a proposal to the National Register of Historic Places. Although the city of Miami Beach sent three representatives to fight against the proposal at a state preservation board hearing in 1979, the designation was unanimously approved. It was the youngest twentieth-century district to be added to the National Register and, at a mile square, one of the largest, containing over four hundred significant examples of buildings designed in Spanish Mediterranean and

Miami Beach, 1977. Photograph by Joel Meyerowitz.

various Art Deco styles. The Art Deco District, as it came to be called, lies between Fifth and Twenty-third streets on the north and south, and is bounded by the Atlantic on the east and Lenox Avenue, near Biscayne Bay, on the west.

Historic preservation is a relatively new idea in this country; it has grown a lot since the sixties, when the National Historic Preservation Act put government funds behind the idea that preservation was important. In most American cities, "new" means "improved," and protecting old buildings has often been a hard-won battle. In Miami Beach, where "old" meant last year's hotel and old people, and where the buildings being saved were younger by a number of years than the woman who championed them, preservation was almost high-concept.

Poor old Miami Beach—at the same time its glossy redevelopment project was sinking, Miami was enjoying an enormous influx of South American capital. As the city fathers watched a glittering new skyline rise up across the bay, their own town grew beige and shabby. Preservation! It seemed like nothing but a liability. In fact, the Art Deco District turned out to be a lifesaver thrown to a city swimming frantically to stay afloat.

REGENERATION

The seventies were bad, but the early eighties were even worse. There was an increase in crime and an exodus of Miami Beach natives to neighboring Broward and Palm Beach counties (the Beach had 60,000 registered voters in 1977; 37,000 in 1987). When Mel Mendelson ran for mayor in 1985, his campaign slogan summed up many people's feelings about the Beach: *Enough Already!*

Everyone had an opinion about What Killed the Beach. The American plan killed the Beach because it kept everyone in the hotels and knocked out restaurants and nightclubs. Wom-

en's lib killed the Beach because it made cheesecake photos obsolete. Success killed the Beach. Jet planes killed the Beach. Castro killed the Beach. Naming streets after celebrities killed the Beach. The failure of the gambling referendum killed the Beach. No pride in service killed the Beach. Old age killed the Beach. Greed killed the Beach. The world shrank.

But even as people lamented the Beach's demise, small but delicately hopeful signs of life began to appear. Capitman was energetically promoting the Deco district, and her son Andrew bought seven hotels on or near Ocean Drive to rehabilitate. A new young crowd gathered at the café on the porch of the Cardozo Hotel, coexisting peacefully with the lawn-chair set. Horowitz began to design color schemes for the buildings, most of which were painted in drab earth tones, which would bring out their geometric forms. One hotel accepted his advice, then another. The new pastel palette got the official seal of approval when the Friedman Bakery, dolled up in candy pink, mint green, and lavender, made the cover of *Progressive Architecture.* Although some people thought the buildings should be treated in a more authentic manner—white with pastel highlights—the new interpretations won popular approval, much as San Francisco's brightly painted Victorian houses have. If there was still any debate that Art Deco was a trend to be reckoned with, *Miami Vice*, broadcast between 1984 and 1988, put it to rest. The show's location scouts fell in love with the district's graphic, high-style architecture and ice-creamy colors. Miami Beach, albeit strewn with dead bodies, was once again being beamed into the nation's living rooms. (No Don Johnson Boulevard yet.)

Publicity for the Art Deco District started to snowball. Articles about the area appeared in all the hip young American and European magazines. Fashion photographers discovered that the light and the beach were as good for photographing bathing suits and spring-catalog clothing as they were in the Caribbean, and Florida had Fed Ex. Tourists and young renters trickled in . . . and the real-estate developers were not far behind.

The Life and Times of Miami Beach

Since the late eighties, the rehabilitation of both Miami Beach's streets and reputation has proceeded at an extraordinary pace. Old-timers who had once derided the "Deco scam" were soon dragging visitors down to show them the miracle that had befallen old South Beach. Within a few years, people stopped talking about What Killed the Beach and started muttering that The Beach Was Being Ruined. A vanguard is always ready to announce that The Beach Is Over. But the waning of this latest revival seems to be some time off. A large part of the city's current allure, in addition to the picturesque architecture, the sun, the sea, and the sand, is that it is a work in progress, a happening. And there is still plenty of territory on Miami Beach waiting to be reclaimed.

Lenny Bruce once said that Miami Beach is where neon went to die, but in fact it's enjoying a spectacular reincarnation. The old hotels have plugged their signs back in; at night, Ocean Drive gleams in pink, lavender, and ice blue. Over on the beach at Lummus Park, the brilliance and clatter of the street's carnival atmosphere melts away. At a distance, the neon lights shining between the dark silhouettes of the palms soften into a romantic haze. It is an artificial sunset, but a gorgeous one.

Bibliography

In addition to the following books and articles, I referred to articles and advertisements in the Miami *News*, the Miami *Herald*, *The New York Times*, and the *Jewish Daily Forward*; issues of the *Society Pictorial*, published in Miami Beach in the 1920s and 1930s; The Carl Graham Fisher papers at the library of the Historical Association of South Florida, as well as pamphlets and brochures there and at the University of Miami Richter Library archives; scrapbooks at the Miami-Dade Public Library; maps from the New York Public Library; and zoning ordinances for the city of Miami Beach.

BOOKS

Albrecht, Donald. *Designing Dreams.* New York: Harper and Row, 1986.

Allen, Frederick Lewis. *Only Yesterday.* New York: Harper and Row, 1931.

Allman, T. D. *Miami, City of the Future.* New York: Atlantic Monthly Press, 1987.

Amory, Cleveland. *The Last Resorts.* New York: Harper and Brothers, 1952.

Ballinger, Kenneth. *Miami Millions.* Miami: Franklin Press, 1936.

Blandings, Don. *Floridays.* New York: Dodd, Mead, 1946.

Buchanan, Edna. *The Corpse Had a Familiar Face.* New York: Random House, 1987.

Capitman, Barbara Baer. *Deco Delights.* New York: E. P. Dutton, 1988.

Chandler, David Leon. *Henry Flagler.* New York: Macmillan, 1986.

Charteris, Leslie. *The Saint in Miami.* Garden City, N.Y.: Sun Dial Press, 1942.

Coon, Horace. *101 American Vacations.* New York: Doubleday, Doran and Company, 1940.

Curl, Donald W. *Mizner's Florida.* Cambridge, Mass.: MIT Press, 1984.

Douglas, Marjory Stoneman. *Florida: The Long Frontier.* New York: Harper and Row, 1967.

———. *Voice of the River.* Englewood, Fla.: Pineapple Press, 1987.

Duncan, Alastair. *Art Deco.* London: Thames and Hudson, 1988.

End, Henry. *Hotels and Motor Hotels.* New York: Whitney Library of Design, 1963.

Federal Writers' Project. *The WPA Guide to Florida: The Federal Writers' Project to 1930s Florida.* New York: Pantheon Books, 1984.

Fisher, Jane. *Fabulous Hoosier.* New York: Robert M. McBride, 1947.

Fox, Charles Donald. *The Truth About Florida.* New York: Simon and Schuster, 1925.

Glazer, Nathan. *American Judaism,* 2nd ed. Chicago: University of Chicago Press, 1989.

Gragert, Steven K., ed. *How to Be Funny and Other Writings of Will Rogers.* Stillwater, Okla.: Oklahoma State University Press, 1983.

Hatton, Hap. *Tropical Splendor.* New York: Alfred A. Knopf, 1987.

Heldt, Henning. "Miami: Heaven or Honky Tonk?" In *Our Fair City,* edited by Robert S. Allen. New York: Vanguard Press, 1947.

Hine, Thomas. *Populuxe.* New York: Alfred A. Knopf, 1986.

Horwitz, Elinor. "Jewish Poverty Hurts in South Beach." In *A Coat of Many Colors,* edited by Abraham D. Lavender. Westport, Conn.: Greenwood Press, 1977.

Hoyt, Edwin P. *A Gentleman of Broadway: The Story of Damon Runyon.* Boston: Little, Brown, 1964.

Jackle, John A. *The Tourist: Travel in Twentieth-Century North America.* Lincoln, Nebr.: University of Nebraska Press, 1985.

Kanfer, Stefan. *A Summer World.* New York: Farrar, Straus and Giroux, 1989.

Kasson, John F. *Amusing the Million: Coney Island at the Turn of the Century.* New York: Hill and Wang, 1978.

Kefauver, Estes. *Crime in America.* Garden City, N.Y.: Doubleday and Company, 1951.

King, Larry. *Tell It to the King.* New York: Putnam, 1988.

Bibliography

Kleinberg, Howard. *Miami: The Way We Were.* Miami: Miami Daily News, 1985.

Kobler, John. *Capone.* New York: Putnam, 1971.

Kofoed, Jack. *Moon Over Miami.* New York: Random House, 1955.

Lapidus, Morris. *An Architecture of Joy.* Miami: E. A. Seemann, 1979.

Liebman, Malvina, and Seymour B. Liebman. *Jewish Frontiersmen.* Miami Beach: Jewish Historical Society of South Florida, 1980.

Lummus, J. N. *The Miracle of Miami Beach.* Miami: Miami Post Publishing Company, 1940.

Mehling, Harold. *The Most of Everything.* New York: Harcourt, Brace and Company, 1960.

Messick, Hank. *Syndicate in the Sun.* New York: Macmillan, 1968.

Metropolitan Dade County Office of Community and Economic Development, Historic Preservation Division. *From Wilderness to Metropolis.* Miami: Metropolitan Dade County Office of Community and Economic Development, 1982.

Miami Beach Improvement Company. *The Bridge, from the Magic City to Beach of Mid Winter Bathing, Miami Beach.* Miami Beach: Miami Beach Improvement Company, 1915–1916.

Muir, Helen. *Miami, U.S.A.* Coconut Grove, Fla.: Hurricane House Publishers, 1953.

Olson, Arlene R. *A Guide to the Architecture of Miami Beach.* Miami: Dade Heritage Trust, 1978.

Parks, Arva Moore. *Miami: The Magic City.* Tulsa, Okla.: Continental Heritage Press, 1981.

Pearce, Donn. *Dying in the Sun.* New York: Charterhouse Books, 1974.

Rabkin, Sol. "How to Keep Exclusive." In *Barriers,* edited by N. C. Belth. New York: Friendly House Publishers, 1958.

Redford, Polly. *The Billion Dollar Sandbar.* New York: E. P. Dutton, 1970.

Root, Keith. *Miami Beach Art Deco Guide.* Miami Beach: Miami Design Preservation League, 1987.

Rothchild, John. *Up for Grabs.* New York: Viking, 1985.

Sheskin, Ira M. *Demographic Study of the Greater Miami Jewish Community.* Miami: Greater Miami Jewish Federation, 1984.

Smiley, Nixon. *Yesterday's Miami.* Miami: E. A. Seemann, 1979.

Smith, Valene L., ed. *Hosts and Guests.* Philadelphia: University of Pennsylvania Press, 1977.

Weigall, T. H. *Boom in Florida.* New York: Alfred H. King, 1932.

Wilson, Edmund. *Red, Black, Blond and Olive.* New York: Oxford University Press, 1949.

Winkler, Revy, and Peg Savage Grey. *Sex and the Senior Citizen.* New York: Frederick Fell, 1968.

Zieman, Irving. *Miami Beach in Rhyme.* Boston: Meador Publishing, 1954.

ARTICLES

Ash, Agnes. "Everybody Gamboled at Cook's Casino." *Miami News,* 20 March 1966, p. 18.

———. "Fastest Way to Score Among Beach Crowd." *Miami News,* 28 March 1965, p. 28.

Ator, Joseph. "We Bet Five Billion." *Chicago Tribune,* 8 November 1936, sec. 7, p. 7.

Benjamin, Louise Payne. "Travelling Light; Dressing Right." *Ladies' Home Journal,* July 1937, 26.

Biemiller, Carl L. "Miami and the Beach." *Holiday,* December 1946, 38–39, 43–44.

Bliven, Bruce. "Where Ev'ry Prospect Pleases." *New Republic,* 26 March 1924, 116–18.

Brenner, Anita. "All States Feed the Streams to Florida." *New York Times,* 24 February 1935, sec. 8, p. 1.

Broun, Heywood. "Miami—A Methodist Mining Camp." *Vanity Fair,* February 1936, 13–15.

Buchanan, Edna. "The Last Days of Al Capone." *Memories,* October/November 1989, 36–40.

Buchanan, Patricia. "Miami's Bootleg Boom." *Tequesta* 30, 1970, 13–24.

Carson, Ruby Leach. "Forty Years of Miami Beach" *Tequesta* 15, 1955, 3–27.

Colum, Padraic. "Miami." *North American Review* 245, no. 1, spring–summer 1938, 135–43.

"Coming On Down." *Time,* 2 April 1965, 41.

"Converting Miami." *Business Week,* 7 March 1942, 26.

"Costly Facelift for an Old Resort." *Time,* 13 August 1979, 52.

"Do We Know There's a War On?" *Look,* 20 March 1945, 28–33.

Dreiser, Theodore. "This Florida Scene: The Future of the Everglades State and Its Great Development Possibilities." *Vanity Fair,* July 1926, 63, 94, 96.

———. "This Florida Scene: Some Meretricious Phrases in the Exploitation of America's Playground." *Vanity Fair,* May 1926, 51, 100, 110.

———. "This Florida Scene: Some Unusual Social Aspects of the Newly Exploited Everglades State." *Vanity Fair,* June 1926, 43, 98, 100.

"Ebb Tide at Miami Beach." *Time,* 19 December 1977, 83.

"The Gold Coast." *Cosmopolitan,* April 1957, 45–47.

Bibliography

Gordon, Barbara. "Everyone Should Have a Summer of '72." *Saturday Review,* 20 May 1972, 24–26.

Greve, Frank. "Florida's Great Gamble." *Miami Herald Tropic Magazine,* 1 June 1975, 10–13, 36–38.

Grossman, Cathy. "Renewal Plans Leave Little Room for Old." *Miami Herald,* 27 March 1974, p. 1B.

Henry, Bruce. "The Gentry Eats Crabs." *Esquire,* February 1939, 44, 135–36.

Hiatt, Walter S. "Crowd Wanderlust." *Century Monthly Magazine,* July 1927, 328–33.

"Human Flotsam of the Florida Hurricane." *Literary Digest,* 9 October 1926, 40–48.

Irace, Fulvio. "Tropical Deco." *Abitare,* July–August 1989, 212–13.

"Is the Bloom Coming off Florida's Boom?" *U.S. News and World Report,* 18 July 1960, 56–58.

Jones, Clarence, and James Savage. "Fontainebleau: Mob Money's Beach Prize." *Miami Herald,* 30 January 1967, p. 1A.

Kefauver, Estes. "What I Found Out About the Miami Mob." *Saturday Evening Post,* 17 April 1951, p. 24.

Kleinberg, Howard. "Beach Row Welcomed Magnates." *Miami News,* 14 March 1987, p. 4C.

———. "Checkered History of Old Deauville." *Miami News,* 21 November 1987, p. 4C.

———. "Cox Tried to Drive Al Capone Away." *Miami News,* 18 June 1983, p. 4C.

———. "Dredge Created First Two Isles in Bay." *Miami News,* 15 February 1986, p. 4C.

———. "Espanola Way Roney's Idea." *Miami News,* 23 June 1984, p. 4C.

———. "The Multi-Millionaire of Star Island." *Miami News,* 23 November 1985, p. 4C.

———. "When Polo Lured Social Set to Beach." *Miami News,* 5 November 1988, p. 4C.

Kobler, John. "Capone: Miami's Model Snowbird." *Miami Herald Tropic Magazine,* 12 September 1971, 9–10, 42.

———. "Roughing It at Miami Beach." *Saturday Evening Post,* 23 February 1957, pp. 19–21, 114, 116–17.

Lapham, Lewis. "Swinging in the City of Illusion." *Saturday Evening Post,* 26 February 1966, pp. 25–31.

Laytner, Ron. "Jane Fisher from Millions to Medicare." *Miami Herald Tropic Magazine,* 29 September 1968.

"Lincoln Road." *Life,* 24 February 1941, 73–79.

"Magic Miamis Study Economics." *Business Week,* 22 March 1941, 38–40.

Maloney, John. "Repelled at Miami Beachhead." *Collier's,* 7 April 1945, 11–13..

Margolies, John. "Morris Lapidus." *Progressive Architecture,* September 1970, 118–23.

Mayer, Martin. "The Man Who Put the Rhinestones on Miami Beach." *Harper's,* March 1965, 61–68.

McCarthy, Joe. "The Man Who Invented America's Winter Playground." *American Heritage,* December 1975, 67–71, 100–101.

McCormick, Anne O'Hare. "Main Street, Too, Winters in Florida." *New York Times,* February 22, 1925, sec. 4, p. 3.

"Miami." *Life,* 29 December 1947, 31–42.

"Miami Beach: Dream Dump, U.S.A." *Architectural Forum,* August 1959, 130–33.

"Miami Beach Idyll." *Glamour,* April 1958, 73–79.

"Miami the Mighty." *Nation,* 12 August 1925, 183.

"Miami Worries About Another Boom." *Life,* 12 February 1945, 63–66.

"Midas' Return." *Time,* 28 February 1944, 23.

Miller, Gene. "Bitter 'Kickback War' Seethes on Beach." *Miami Herald,* 19 April 1959.

Miller, Susan, and Joseph P. Averill. "Miami Beach: A Steel and Concrete Shore." *Miami Herald,* 24 May 1970, p. 1A.

Millstein, Gilbert. "Architect De Luxe of Miami Beach." *New York Times Magazine,* 6 January 1957, 26–28, 38, 42.

Mohl, Raymond A. "Shadows in the Sunshine: Race and Ethnicity in Miami." *Tequesta* 49, 1989, 63–80.

Nazario, Sonia L. "Miami Beach Courting Younger People As It Tries to Shed Retirement Image." *Wall Street Journal,* 8 October 1985, p. 33.

"Pleasure Dome." *Time,* 19 February 1940, 18–21.

"Pleasure Domes and Pastrami." *Newsweek,* 12 August 1968, 20–25.

Randolph, Nancy. "Gold-Lined Pocketbooks at Miami." *Palm Beach Post,* 4 March 1940.

"Revels in Florida Assailed by Pastor." *New York Times,* 9 March 1925, p. 20.

Richard, Melvin J. "Tidelands and Riparian Rights in Florida." *Miami Law Quarterly* 3, no. 3, April 1949, 339–64.

Rogers, Will. "Carl Took Florida from the Alligators and Gave It to the Indianians." *Tulsa Daily World,* 11 October 1925.

Runyon, Damon. "The Brighter Side." *New York American,* 14 May 1937.

———. "Runyon Has Too Much Sand in His Shoes to Make Trip to

Bibliography

Hollywood." *New York American,* 13 October 1936.

Sherrill, Robert. "The All-Too-American City." *New York Times Magazine,* 4 August 1968, 7, 9, 34, 36, 38, 40, 43, 44, 50, 54.

Sosin, Milt. "Negroes Shun Beach Hotel, Fear Threats." *Miami Daily News,* 5 May 1953, p. 1A.

"South Miami Beach: Living in the Ruins." *Newsweek,* 11 April 1982, 10.

"Stage Set." *New Yorker,* 25 December 1954, 47–48.

Sutton, Horace. "Ah, Fla." *Saturday Review,* 13 February 1954, 44–47.

———. "Où Est la Suntan Oil de ma Tante?" *Saturday Review,* 8 January 1955, 32–34.

———. "Pole to Pampas." *Saturday Review,* 10 November 1956, 46–47.

———. "We're Not Trying to Impress You." *Saturday Review,* 2 June 1956, 30–31.

Trillin, Calvin. "Reflections of a More or Less Junior Citizen Shopping on Washington Avenue." *New Yorker,* 16 February 1976, 56–59.

"Two Great Resorts—A Candid Look." *Life,* 20 January 1958, 87–94.

Wilson, F. Page. "We Chose the Subtropics." *Tequesta* 12, 1952, 19.

Ziegler, Mel. "Journey's End in a Promised Land." *Miami Herald Tropic Magazine,* 24 November 1968, 11, 13, 14, 17, 18, 20, 44.

Index

Italicized page numbers indicate photographs.

Index

Index

Index

Index

Index

Index

Index

Index

Index

Index

Illustration Credits

Ann Armbruster: pages 102 (bottom), 125, 146, 151

AP/Wide World Photos: page 164

Kenneth Lee Benjamin Collection: pages 73, 90, 168

Bettmann/UPI: pages 70 (right), 71 (bottom), 128 (top), 169 (top), 188

Seth Bramson Collection: pages 15, 18, 24, 29, 39, 60, 97, 122 (bottom)

Dennie Cody: page 177

Ralph Crane/Black Star: pages 117 (top), 118

Randall Cushing: page 116 (all)

Olive Delahunt: page 52

Jerry Driendl/FPG: page 184

Alfred Eisenstadt, *Life* Magazine © 1940 Time Inc.: page 99 (bottom)

Florida Photographic Collections, Florida State Archives: pages 7, 9, 12 (bottom), 13, 14, 45, 109, 148 (top), 153 (top), 159, 174

Fontainebleau Hotel: page 134

Fortune Magazine: pages 62, 70 (left)

Murray Franklin: pages 122 (top), 160

Chris Hansen photo: page 150 (all)

Bill Held photo: page 161 (bottom)

Historical Association of Southern Florida: back of case; pages ii, vi, 3, 5, 6 (top and bottom), 10, 12 (top), 17, 19 (top and bottom), 21 (bottom), 22 (top and bottom), 23 (top and bottom), 26, 27, 30 (top and bottom), 34, 42 (left and right), 44 (top and bottom), 46 (top and bottom), 51, 64 (bottom), 66, 68 (top and bottom), 78, 85 (top and bottom), 96, 98, 101 (top and bottom), 104 (top and bottom), 106 (top), 112, 113, 114 (top and bottom right), 117 (bottom), 119 (top), 121, 123 (top and bottom), 126, 161 (top), 180

Ellen Kunes: page 89 (left and right)

Morris and Alan Lapidus: pages 114 (bottom left), 138, 139, 142, 143, 144, 145 (top and bottom)

John Launois/Black Star: pages 140, 165, 166

Kenneth Laurence: pages 124 (bottom), 202

Darren Lew photo: pages 175, 176

Library of Congress: pages 54, 58, 64 (top), 72, 74, 86, 107

Magnum Photos © Henri Cartier-Bresson: pages 155 (left and right), 156

Daniel F. Malone: pages viii, 4

Joel Meyerowitz photo: page 182

Miami *Herald*: pages 110, 136

Miami *News*: pages 41, 71 (top left and top right), 88, 124 (top), 128 (bottom), 169 (bottom), 181

Aristides Millas Collection: page 105

Gary Monroe photo: page 179 (bottom)

Mount Mercer Inc.: page 137

Terry O'Neill photo: page 172

Jack Ott: pages 16, 130

Arva Moore Parks Collection: pages 20, 21 (top)

Stanley Platkin, from the collection of the late Edward A. Platkin: pages 120 (all), 132

The Raleigh Hotel, Miami: front of case

Alice Rogers: page x

Romer Collection, Miami-Dade Public Library: pages 32, 33, 37, 55, 56, 65, 75, 81, 83, 84 (top and bottom), 91, 119 (bottom)

Hettie Russell: page 102 (top)

Jay Spencer Collection: page 129

Penny Stallings: page 152

Donald H. Sultner-Welles Collection, Archive Center, NMAH, Smithsonian Institution: page 148 (bottom)

Andy Sweet photo: page 179 (top)

Charles Trainor photo, courtesy Stella Trainor: page 153 (bottom)

Carol Unger: page 99 (top)

University of Miami Library: page 106 (bottom)

Rosemary Hubbel Wirkus: page 38

The Mitchell Wolfson, Jr. Collection, Miami Beach, Florida, courtesy the Wolfsonian Foundation: pages 12 (middle), 36 (left and right), 50

Wometco Enterprises: page 158

A Note on the Type

The text of this book was set in a postscript version of Bembo, a well-known Monotype face. Named for Pietro Bembo, the celebrated Renaissance writer and humanist scholar who was made a cardinal and served as secretary to Pope Leo X, the original cutting of Bembo was made by Francesco Griffo of Bologna only a few years after Columbus discovered America.

Sturdy, well balanced, and finely proportioned, Bembo is a face of rare beauty, extremely legible in all of its sizes.

Composed by The Sarabande Press, New York

Printed and bound by Arnoldo Mondadori Editore, Verona, Italy

Designed by Iris Weinstein